John L.C. Mitman

PREMARITAL COUNSELING

A MANUAL FOR CLERGY AND COUNSELORS

THE SEABURY PRESS

Cover design: Art Direction, Inc.

Library of Congress Catalog Card Number: 80-36690
ISBN: 0-86683-879-1
(previously published in hardcover with ISBN: 0-8164-0467-4)

Printed in the United States of America
5   4   3   2   1

The Seabury Press
430 Oak Grove
Minneapolis, Minnesota 55403

Premarital Counseling

To Ruth, my wife
with love and deep gratitude

Acknowledgements

It is a witness to the reality of the body of Christ that this book has taken form. A host of concerned, thoughtful, patient, generous and hard-working Christians have supported and encouraged me during the long process of translating my experience, intuition, scholarship and doubt into the written word.

I offer my deep gratitude to all those who encouraged me to stop talking about this project and do it. Certainly it would never have been possible without the individuals and institutions who provided financial support: The Episcopal Ministry at Michigan State University, the Diocese of Michigan and numerous families.

It was the Chichester Theological College in Sussex, England, which provided the support community in which the bulk of the work was completed during the summer of 1977, an environment without which my motivation and discipline would certainly have flagged.

My grateful thanks to all those who have offered their time and expertise in editing the manuscript: The Rev. Brian Stevenson of the Chichester Theological College; The Rev. Vincent Strudwick of the Society of the Sacred Mission; The Venerable William Logan, Archdeacon of the Diocese of Michigan; The Rev. William A. Eddy, Rector of All Saints, East Lansing, Michigan; The Rev. Earl Brill of Washington, D.C.; Mrs. Dixie Lee Premer, an eagle-eyed editor and friend from Okemos, Michigan; and most of all, Dr. Anne C. Garrison, recently retired from the faculty of Michigan State University, who has given innumerable hours and great encouragement to me over the past year.

My thanks also to Mrs. Bianca Tobin of Chichester and Mrs. Lois Hertzer of East Lansing, who graciously tolerated my tapes, notes and typing while typing the various editions of the manuscript.

And finally to my wife, Ruth, and to our children, Gretchen and Stephan, I give thanks for their support and tolerance, without which I could never have completed this work.

Contents

Preface

The divorce rate in America is approaching fifty percent. Many urban areas are now recording more divorces each year than marriages. This is an astonishing state of affairs when one considers the extraordinary agony which usually accompanies such an event. In addition to the devastation wrought by separation and divorce, our society is crippled by what has happened to the countless people bound in marriages which are unhappy, unfulfilling, painful, debilitating and dehumanizing. There is virtually no one in our society whose life at some time has not been profoundly affected by the trauma of marital difficulties, separation or divorce, either in one's family, or within one's circle of friends, neighbors and business acquaintances. The pain and anguish which are caused by divorce and marital strife are terribly costly to our society in both human and financial terms.

While it is true that the numbers of marriages in the church have declined in recent years, the assertion that marriage will be little more than a quaint anachronism by the turn of the century is to be questioned most seriously. The fact of the matter is that the total number of couples married by the clergy in religious ceremonies appears to be leveling off throughout America. Even Jessie Bernard in *The Future of Marriage* concludes that while the character of the marriage contract may be changing quite radically and moving toward a great variety of models, "The future of marriage is as assured as any social form can be ... people continue to commit themselves to each other."[1]

Whatever the future of marriage may be, people continue to present themselves at church doors to be married; and clergy of various denominations and traditions are virtually the only persons in our society who are called upon with any regularity to provide premarital instruction, counseling or advice. To be sure, the number of hours involved in preparing a couple for marriage is considerable. When one adds together four to six hours of premarital counseling, the time set aside for the rehearsal of the wedding ceremony, the duration of the wedding itself and any social affairs before and after the wedding to which the pastor may be invited (which he may or may not elect to attend), the hours mount up very quickly. The marriage of two people may well require of the counselor/pastor a number of hours equivalent to half of a normal forty-hour working week. Such a time commitment is questioned by many clergy and, in fact, is used as an excuse to avoid this responsibility. However, if the pastor considers the amount of time spent in marital and post-marital counseling dealing with problems and issues which might well have been anticipated before marriage, the need for conscientious premarital counseling programs becomes readily apparent.

More to the point, the church's ministry in pre-marital, marital and post-marital counseling may well be her most crucial pastoral responsibility in our society. It is certainly true that as the divorce rate climbs, there is a sizeable backlog of troubled marriages which must be considered while at the same time there is a greater commitment of time and energy required for premarital counseling. The needs increase at the same time that resources to meet these needs are ever more limited. This is the dilemma: How high a priority should ministry to married persons receive in the church?

Horror stories of ill-prepared and ill-informed premarital counseling abound. There is the clergyman who sets out a cassette tape recorder in a cold room with three hours of taped lectures to which the prospective husband and wife are supposed to listen and from which, presumably, they are to learn all they have to know. There are clergy who literally never lay eyes on a couple until the wedding rehearsal. One pastor told me that he thought the whole enterprise to be a waste of time! He does, however, attempt to meet with a couple six months after their marriage if indeed they are still married and if they are accessible.

The Pre-Cana Conference approach, that is, counseling with groups of couples before marriage, is used quite extensively in the Roman Catholic Church. However, it is the experience of many pastors that a considerable number of issues which should be raised before marriage are difficult or impossible to approach in a group setting. It is recognized that in the United States, with a shortage of clergy and trained laypersons and large numbers of persons seeking to be married within the Roman Catholic Church, the only viable alternative is the Pre-Cana Conference approach. So it is that the Roman Catholic Church has developed the Pre-Cana program as an alternative to the very personalized premarital instruction suggested in this manual. However, there is little or no justification for this group format being used in most non-Roman Catholic churches.

The fact that the pastor may not be married or may never have been married does not preclude his offering not only competent but also helpful advice and counsel before marriage. As a nation, we passed through a period in which it was postulated that if you were not a part of a particular group, race, nationality or social class, you would find it impossible to offer anything—advice, insight, etc.—to aid that segment of society in any way. " Only blacks can help blacks; only Chicanos can help Chicanos; the poor are the ones to help the poor; the oppressed are the only ones to help the oppressed—no one else can relate to their problems or really understand them." Fortunately, we seem to have passed from that mindset to a more liberal and helpful stance. It is only in the last few years that the private letters of John Masefield have been published. An astonishing revelation was that this man who wrote with such love, insight, sensitivity and appreciation of the sea was himself consistently subject to bitter and grotesque seasickness virtually from the moment he stepped onto the dock prior to sailing until well after he had returned to the stability of dry land. As in the case of Masefield, while it may indeed be helpful, it is not necessary for one to have personally experienced a particular state of being in order to acquire and offer a significant understanding of a particular area of life. It is, however, the proven experience of celibate or unmarried clergy or lay counselors that teaming up with a skilled and committed married person or couple may be most helpful in premarital, marital and post-marital counseling. This is certainly not to say that single marriage counselors haven't a definite responsibility to study, read and take advantage of what training courses may be available to them to increase their skills in this important area of ministry. The need for continual study by all people involved in any phase of marriage or personal counseling increases in proportion to the many changes in our society.

Too often, we lose sight of the fact that preparation for holy matrimony is an exciting opportunity for evangelism. Most people presenting themselves for marriage are either vaguely negative in their commitment to the Lord Christ and his church or are at an age where conscientious questioning of belief may be very much in the forefront of their minds. Premarital counseling provides an exciting potential for ministry which far overshadows a similar opportunity which may come in pre-baptismal conferences. The liturgy for the celebration and blessing of a marriage offers a theological statement as well as a dramatic presentation of God's abiding love for his creation. Premarital conferences offer a unique opportunity for the teaching and sharing of the faith of the risen Christ, an occasion which should be celebrated thoughtfully, joyfully and honestly. If we understand grace as the love of God in action, the sacrament of marriage is an extraordinary occasion for interpretation of that same love to those whose need for it at this crucial time in their lives is clearly manifest.

In surveying my own calendar, I realized that I averaged seventeen hours a week in premarital, marital and post-marital counseling. In marital and post-marital counseling sessions, I often found myself saying, "Had you come to me before you were married, I would have urged you to consider the following question. . . ." The invariable response from counselees is, "The clergyman who married us never raised that kind of question."

It is my conviction that the church has failed in its ministry of premarital counseling. The existing materials (books, pamphlets, filmstrips and other curricula) are inadequate. Drawing upon the experience gained in preparing approximately 150 couples for marriage, this volume is intended to offer a practical program for marriage preparation in the hope that it may be helpful to others whether they be laypersons or clergy seeking to carry out this most vital ministry.

While it will be clear throughout that my own background is Anglican, I have attempted to present this program in such a way that it may be as helpful as possible to clergy and laypersons from various theological traditions. Wherever possible I have used the term "pastor" when referring to the counselor. While this word may have specific connotations in some Christian denominations, it is used here to refer to any qualified person, man or woman, ordained or not, who undertakes this ministry.

We would do well to recognize that premarital counseling is one area of pastoral ministry which is virtually impossible to teach in the context of a seminary or alternative theological training course. Even in courses which include extensive field study, it would be a very rare occurrence for ordained clergy to assign a seminarian to prepare a couple for marriage, let alone provide a suitable clinical setting for review of his or her work.

I have attempted to avoid sexist language throughout. However, the limitations of our tongue are manifest in this regard. Suffice it to say that the use of a masculine pronoun or adjective in referring to the counselor (or pastor) or the counselee is to be understood generically.

The bibliography is brief; it is intended as a reading list for the counselor, not as an exhaustive listing of all the works relating to the theological, sociological, psychological, anthropological and historical aspects of the institution of marriage. The works listed are generally available.

This volume is about marriage. Only at the end will we deal with the wedding. It is well to keep in mind the comment of the counselor who said, "For two hours I talked marriage and they only heard wedding."[2]

The program is presented as it has developed over the past fifteen years of my ordained ministry but is by no means offered as the final word: It is not gospel. Rather, it is hoped that it may offer a starting point for some, challenge and enrichment for others.

For the convenience of the reader, the substance of the interviews is presented in outline form in Appendix A.

Some General Thoughts on Counseling

Since I began exercising this ministry of premarital counseling following ordination, I have had many conversations with clergy and laypersons from many traditions concerning this topic. Some of these people are primarily concerned with the demise of the American family, while others seem preoccupied with the theological, philosophical or theoretical questions involved. Many of those with whom I have had lengthy and substantial discussions on premarital and marital counseling have seriously questioned both the intensity and ultimate effectiveness of my approach. The reaction of some to the questions I ask and issues I raise is nothing less than shock. Some believe that I go too far and probe too deeply. Concurrently, some assume that the feedback I receive is of questionable value for the process of preparing people for marriage. I am asked, "How do you know that people are being honest with you? How can you ferret out the gamesplayers, those who have read all the books and are simply regurgitating the answers they feel you want to hear? Are you simply using human need and the mandate of the church to satisfy your own need to be needed?" Others take a different tack: "How do you know, in fact, that such an extensive program in premarital counseling is effective? And, even assuming the effectiveness of the approach and the program as a whole, what makes it work? What makes you think you're a good counselor, if, in fact, you are?"

I do not find responding to these questions an easy task. However, I do have an obligation to the reader and to myself to attempt a response.

In preparing these reflections, I have come to realize just how indebted I am to the work of Carl Rogers. I would be most reluctant to characterize myself as a Rogerian, as the works of Carl Jung and others have had a profound effect upon my person and ministry. However, upon examination I find that my starting point in premarital counseling closely parallels Rogers' general approach to counseling. His assumption is that the greatest human need is for each person to recognize and accept his own value, worth and significance. Because he recognizes this as the primary need of the person, he approaches each counselee with the attitude that each person is indeed valued, that each person is of worth and that each person is of significance in this world. The concomitant reality is that because each person is significant, worthwhile and of value, he is, with assistance, capable of working out his own problems drawing upon his inimitable resources.[3] Hence, I favor the nondirective approach traditionally associated with the Rogerian tradition.

While Rogers' philosophy of therapy is based upon secular humanistic assumptions about the nature of man, I would see the value of the person based upon the fact that each person is a beloved child of God, a creation for which God wants the very best, the most loving and fulfilling life possible. With Rogers, I would say that how we approach premarital counseling is not determined by technique or method. Our approach is determined by the application of a philosophy of human understanding in which the good counselor seeks to understand *with* the person rather than to emphasize the analytical approach which is to understand *about*.[4] As a christian, where Rogers would use the word philosophy, I would use theology, the *theo-logos* as it relates to persons in relationship, in this case, the marital relationship.

With this theological understanding as the starting point, the premarital counselor begins by treating those who come to him as persons, individually and as part of a couple, who are of the same inestimable value to the pastor as they are to the God who created them. If such an attitude is genuine—without being unctuous—the pastor can reasonably expect the prospective bride and groom to respond to issues and questions with all the candor and understanding which is theirs to exercise. Such an expectation is not limited to matters which the pastor may introduce; the counselees are likewise enabled to deal with their own feelings as they formulate and develop their own questions and understanding regarding themselves and the marital love relationship.

While there are many, many questions to be asked and issues to be raised, from the beginning it is the pastor's responsibility to establish the fact that he is a good listener, that he will respect both party's feelings as he hopes that they will respect his and that his role is not to sit in judgment on their past behavior, their thoughts or their feelings. As a professional group, clergy have difficulty with silence. The ministry is a verbally-oriented vocation. Sitting in silence, allowing people to think and be, is difficult for many ministers, whether or not they are ordained. It is nevertheless crucial to the counseling ministry and is equally necessary in premarital counseling, if not more so. Caveat: Ministry in silence must never become a game of "chicken" in which the object is to stare the other person down. A gentle silence conveys respect and offers a context for growth.

The pastor must convince the bride and groom of his commitment to confidentiality. To violate the confidence established with the couple is to violate the person, to devalue the person in the midst of a process in which the primary ground rule is that the person is unique and of inestimable value in the eyes of God and the church.

A major problem facing the pastor in premarital counseling is gamesplaying and untruthful responses. If the pastor is sensitive to the tone of the conversation and takes care to note inconsistencies and contradictions in the responses and reflections of the couple, he should be able to recognize times when the prospective bride and groom are not being truthful with him and each other. However, we must recognize that some people are quite skilled at this type of gamesmanship. Smugness and passivity may be hostility in another guise. This type of response should be faced squarely with the couple. More important is the question, at whom is this hostility directed? Is it toward the pastor, the church, the proposed partner, the families or themselves? If after the matter is investigated it becomes clear that the hostility or anger is directed toward the proposed partner or toward the self, the advisability of the marriage must be questioned. Marriage is no answer to deep-seated anger; marriage only offers yet another context in which it may be expressed.

An approach to the question of whether the prospective bride and groom are being honest with the pastor and with themselves may be found in the development of a sense of mutuality. That is, if the well-prepared pastor can communicate his respect for and belief in the value of the two people and their proposed marriage, they in turn come to value the pastor as a caring, competent counselor, a person whom they would not wish to hurt. If we are all in this enterprise together, to lie to one's pastor or to withhold feelings is more accurately described as cheating on oneself, one's partner and the marriage. There is nothing to gain from such behavior and a great deal to lose. The break in the gamesplaying comes when the future bride and groom realize that the pastor sees as much or even greater value and significance in them than they see in themselves. My experience is that remarkable candor is not only possible but probable in such an atmosphere.

However, in the final analysis, neither the pastor nor the two engaged people can know for sure whether or not they are being truthful, whether or not they are consciously or unconsciously playing games. As a dear friend once said, "Discussion in marriage preparation sessions is not necessarily the same as preparation for marriage; a tree planted by the river of water is not necessarily seriously committed to an extended course in how to grow."

Three issues remain. The first is that the nature of the premarital counseling task dictates that the pastor be both therapist and teacher. In nearly all cases, the active pastor knows more about marriage, its potential and pitfalls, than the couple does. From our reading and experience of dealing with troubled marriages, we should at least be able to identify and verbalize the primary questions which relate to the marital relationship. As individual problems or problems in the relationship are identified, the role of the therapist predominates. At times during the interview the pastor clearly becomes the teacher, one who shares his knowledge, experience and wisdom with the couple. While it is essential to recognize the existence of this dual role, it is nearly impossible to separate the two functions.

The second issue is that while the pastor must accept the people presenting themselves to be married as people of worth, valued in the sight of God and his church, he should not fail to recognize and to attempt to reconcile a person who has done wrong or is doing wrong. The message of the gospel is one of reconciliation with God, with the rest of God's creation and with oneself. The person may recognize a moral problem and feel guilty. He may fail to recognize a moral problem and feel guilty. Or he may acknowledge the wrong and avoid dealing with the guilt. The pastor must not allow himself to subjugate his understanding of Christian ethics to his image as Mr. Nice Guy. A very common situation relating to such a dilemma is that many of the couples who seek to be married today are living together before marriage. What is the pastor's position on this matter? How can the pastor maintain his own sense of integrity and at the same time create a positive pastoral relationship with the couple? A more subtle issue comes to mind: What of the ethical problems involved in the manner in which bride and groom treat one another? Dehumanizing behavior is just as prevalent among brides and grooms as among the population as a whole. Returning to our first principle, if we begin with the premise that each person is of intrinsic value and observe potential marriage partners treating one another as people of little or no value, where and how do we bring our ethical standards to bear? This is an instance in which the pastor is both therapist, as he leads the person to an understanding of his or her dehumanizing behavior, and priest, as he leads the person to a recognition of the need for penitence and carries out his ministry of reconciliation. The problem becomes, how does one convince another of the importance of his or her dehumanizing behavior without talking down to the person, dehumanizing him or her in the process? One must be prepared to state, "I value you as a person, a child of God; but I cannot accept the things you are doing as being right in the eyes of God."

The third issue which calls for some discussion is the fact that this whole program depends in large part upon the ability of people to express themselves verbally. While verbal facility is not the hallmark of a successful marriage, it certainly makes the pastor's task easier in premarital counseling. With the exception of the one rather extraordinary example mentioned in the afterword, I have always found those who come to me to be able to verbalize adequately. The problem comes not in the person's ability to express himself or herself but in the quality or accuracy of the verbalizations. This difficulty is but another expression of gamesmanship, untruthfulness and hostility, the problems discussed above. Finally, if the problem lies in the distinction between one's ability and one's willingness to respond verbally, the pastor might be well-advised to return to an assessment of his ability or inability to communicate to the couple his belief in their worth in his eyes and in the eyes of God, the basis on which his pastoral relationship and effectiveness depend.

:1:

Theological Considerations

Katheryn Kuhlman used to begin most of her sermons with the statement, "I believe in miracles." Whatever one may think of Miss Kuhlman and her ministry, her opening chorus let her congregation know from the onset what she believed and, more specifically, that she believed in what she was saying and in what she was doing. Anyone who engages in premarital counseling must understand, decide and declare how he feels about marriage.

A recent issue of *Punch* carried a cartoon which pictured a standard cocktail party with a crowd gathered about a particularly smug-looking young man. A woman was speaking to another in the foreground and the caption read, "He's a well-known psychiatrist who believes that mental illness should be encouraged. This has made him a contemporary cult hero."[1] In an age of cult heroes who bask in the light generated by the focus of popular attention on extreme positions, it is perfectly possible for people who have no understanding of or commitment to marriage, as it is traditionally understood, to seek to function as premarital counselors.

As Jesus asked Peter, "Who do you say that I am?", each of us must ask himself whether he believes in this reality called marriage before he can hope to prepare anyone for it or be of any assistance to those who are experiencing marital difficulties.

While to speak or write of marriage as being an out-of-date, chauvinistic, dehumanizing, fascist institution is very much in vogue at the moment, many of those who defend marriage in theological or secular spheres seem to do so in quite negative terms as rather paranoid defenders of a historic institution. Instead of beginning by affirming the gift of a relationship which through the love of God may be a community of grace, the negative effect of such a starting point is never overcome. God preserve us from this gainsaying generation!

How then shall we proceed? This is to be a practical manual in marriage preparation. It is not within the purview of this work to provide an exhaustive examination of the history of marriage in the Judeo-Christian tradition. Nor is it possible to examine the contemporary theories of marriage in any detail. Nevertheless, some history and theology must be reviewed in order that we may better understand the tradition on which we base this ministry of preparing persons for Christian marriage.

To be sure, there are a great many ill-founded suppositions about marriage. From the time of Constantine, the church has labored under the misapprehension that what the church believed and taught was accepted in what was, in reality, primarily a secular society. It may certainly be said that the church valued marriage and attributed to those who were married at least a recognition of the fact of marriage. However, until quite recently, marriage was reserved for those who could satisfy two criteria: a household had to be provided and the man had to have a proven source of income to support a wife and family.[2] While these conditions for marriage were generally understood, they did not prevent liaisons between men and women. As might be expected, children were conceived. The result was extended family households. In fact, conception followed by marriage became a way for couples who wished to be married to force the issue, as it were, and marry even if the economics of the age failed to provide a household and employment to support the family. Examination of the dates of marriages and baptisms in parish records throughout Europe establishes this fact. The church never settled on a liturgy for marriage until the early thirteenth century. It was not until the Council of Trent that the sacramental character of marriage was finally set down. The idea of the nuptial mass, save for the very rich and powerful, is of much more recent origin.*

Prior to the rise of the middle class, marriage was a continuing historical reality—but only for those who could afford it. We have the extraordinary anomaly of the church seeming to forget the teachings of Jesus and Saint Paul in the face of the social and economic pressures of the times. Therefore, before we claim to understand the challenges to marriage in our present age, we should look far more carefully at how the church has understood marriage in the past and how it has applied that understanding. Can we take for granted the strength of the tradition?

More important than the above for the Christian is what the scriptures record of what our Lord and his followers said about marriage. Tradition may inform scripture and practice may test its viability; yet scripture must remain the basis of our understanding and teaching as Christians with regard to marriage, as to all other areas of our life experience. Unfortunately, many of the exegeses on the texts of scripture which relate to marriage have been done in the context of examining, defending or attacking divorce and remarriage within the church. Such an approach deals primarily with the unfortunate ending of marriage and lacks the clear, strong tone of affirmation which we prefer as the basis of the teaching of the church.

As much as we would like it to be so, the Old and New Testament teachings on exclusivity and permanence in the man-woman relationship are not consistent. For instance, Jacob took four wives, Leah, Rachel, and the maidservants of each. Esau had at least five wives, while Abraham had two wives and an

---

* For an exhaustive study of both the secular and religious history of marriage, I would suggest three books. The earlier chapters of Jessie Bernard's *The Future of Marriage* are extremely helpful from the secular point of view. Jack Dominian, a Roman Catholic psychiatrist from Britain, rather bridges the ecclesiastical-secular gap with his work, *Christian Marriage: The Challenge of Change* (note the subtitle). Finally, the definitive historical work from the ecclesiastical side is D. Sherwin Bailey's, *The Man-Woman Relation in Christian Thought*. This volume was published in America as the *Sexual Relation in Christian Thought*. The variation in title is an interesting commentary on the perception of editors, marketers and readers in Britain and the United States. Suffice it to say, all three books establish the low regard in which marriage has been held until recent years. Holy matrimony was not always understood to be all that honorable an estate.

unrecorded number of concubines. Most illuminating to this study is the story of Jacob (Gen. 25:19ff). This extraordinary Old Testament character's love for Rachel (for whom he lived in servitude for seven years) prefigures a God-encouraged drive for a monogamous relationship: The emergence of the person *most special*. Rachel is to Jacob far more than a favorite wife. In Jacob's relationship to Rachel we see a union in joyous intimacy with one person. It is this type of relationship which we find more explicitly set forth in the New Testament.

Yet another clear and dramatic contrast between the Old and New Testaments is seen in the practice of levirate marriage (Deut. 25:5-10) in which a man weds his brother's widow and fathers children. This practice accomplishes two ends: It satisfies the imperative, "Be fruitful and multiply . . ." (Gen. 1:28) and assures the inheritance of both name (an expression of eternal life) and property. Jesus' teaching ignores such practices. Finally, Jesus disallows the writ of divorce provided by Moses.

The New Testament passages which relate to marriage are quite limited: Mark 10: 1-12, its Synoptic parallels (Matthew 19: 1-12; and Luke 16: 18); Mark 12:18-27 and parallels (Matthew 22:23-33 and Luke 20:27-40); St. Paul, writing in his first letter to the Corinthians (7: 10-16 and 13: 1-13), to the Romans (7: 2-3), and to the Ephesians (5: 22-33); and the passage referred to in the "Introduction to the Solemnization of Holy Matrimony" of *The Book of Common Prayer,* that is, the wedding in Cana of Galilee (John 2: 1-11).

In the first set of Synoptic passages, the elements of Jesus' teaching on marriage seem clear. First, though the question was framed in the context of divorce and remarriage, by saying, "What God hath joined together let no man put asunder," Jesus asserts that God is directly involved in the marriage as the one who joins the one person to the other. Second, the prohibition against adultery underscores the exclusive nature of the marriage bond: There may be for each no other. Third, this bond of marriage is for life, except for cases of adultery. We note that there is substantial agreement between Mark and Matthew, while Luke preserves only a very brief comment concerning divorce and adultery in a quite different context.

Modern biblical criticism, particularly form-criticism, places these passages in considerable doubt. This is especially true of the sections of the passages in which Jesus addresses the disciples in private. Such excursuses are thought by many to be later additions by editors whose intention was to clarify what Jesus really meant by what they were certain he had said.

Perhaps it can be agreed only that Jesus said, "Those whom God hath joined together . . . ," as this would be the central teaching of the passages and refers quite clearly to Genesis 2: 22-24. In this most extreme view, we are left with only God's involvement in marriage, while exclusivity and permanence are unsubstantiated. And yet, what more could we ask as assurance of both the sanctity of marriage and the most powerful resource to make of it all it may be—exclusive and permanent?

The second set of Synoptic passages records the Sadducees' questioning Jesus on the result of serial monogamy on earth and family life in the resurrection. In these passages, Jesus points us toward the realization that in this present age marriage is an institution necessary for the propagation and nurture of the human race and for *order* in daily life. Jesus makes clear that such questions are made moot in the resurrection. There is no marriage in the Kingdom because there is no need for license to cohabit. He leads the Sadducees out of legalism into the vision of a union, a concept of bonding in glory of men and women as asexual beings—angels (Mark 12:25). It is important to note that marriage is a concept that was imposed by the state, not by God. Even though we are likely to use the words interchangeably, *matrimony* (the divine sanctioning of a relationship) and *marriage* (the legal sanctioning of pairing) are not the same, and holy bonding supersedes both.

St. Paul presents the believer with a variety of problems while at the same time affirming the basic teaching of Jesus. When we recall that Paul antedates Mark, the authenticity of the teaching on marriage recorded in the Synoptics is at once enhanced. However, two realities must be kept in mind with regard to Paul's teaching. First, he wrote in the expectation of the imminent second coming of Christ to communities he was attempting to nurture until the eschaton. This affects all his writings; and while such recognition does not invalidate his teaching, it casts it in a particular context which must be seriously confronted. Second, much of Paul's teaching is difficult to accept in an age in which the church as well as society is coming to appreciate women as people of equal value and stature with men. It is not only the male who was created in the image of God any more than it was only Adam who dwelt in harmony, acceptance and openness with God in the garden. We see in Paul's letter to the Corinthians the exceptions made for those whose spouses were pagans. Clearly, Paul responded to specific questions which had been put to him, at times distinguishing between what he understood Jesus to have taught and what he himself felt appropriate in the particular circumstances.

Paul was a pastor, a chief pastor of the post-ascension community. We are left with what he wrote in response to questions which are not necessarily ours. But we are also left with the totality of the church's scripture, tradition and experience. We are called upon to apply all that body of knowledge to those for whom we have a pastoral responsibility within the same Body of Christ of which Paul was a chief pastor for his time. We cannot simply ask Jesus or write Paul to get the answers. It remains that we are the Body along with all of those who have gone before. If so, we must assume the implied responsibilities.

With regard to marriage, as opposed to divorce and remarriage, the primary contemporary use of St. Paul is the passage in the letter to the Ephesians (5: 22-33) in which he makes the statement, "wives, be subject to your husbands." As a member incorporate of the Body of Christ and as one who seeks to understand and apply the whole of the Christian faith, it is my judgment that the submission imperative of Paul is simply inconsistent with the gospel message. On the one hand, we are called upon to proclaim freedom to the captives; and on the other, Paul directs submission of wives to husbands without any provisions for extenuating circumstances. The contrast of the great hymn of love in I Corinthians 13 (the context of which is the body of Christ, not Christian marriage as may be suggested by its frequent use in nuptial liturgies) and the heavy-handed analogy of husband and wife to the Lord Christ and the church is overwhelming and, in the end, devastating.

While I do not believe that the Ephesians passage can be reconciled to the gospel message, I do believe that it can be understood. If one can accept the "submit yourselves" teaching as a short-termed expedient answer to the question of the ordering of domestic relations until the eschaton, it makes some sense. We would do well to recall that for all Paul's godly wisdom, his credentials in domestic relations are nowhere established. Again, Paul spoke as a man of his culture, as a zealous convert with what he thought to be a clear view of the eschatological horizon to people who had addressed specific questions to him.

In the end, Paul's contribution is in witnessing to the synoptic tradition and the great gift of the hymn in I Corinthians 13.

In both the Old and New Testament traditions, an unstated but critical question lurks in the background: If a wife is adulterous, how can the husband be certain about the true identity of his son and heir, a most important question to a Jewish father? However, increasingly, Christendom has come to view marriage as a context for fulfillment of husband, wife and children: a view consistent with the totality of the gospel message but which inevitably casts both Old and New Testament theology in a new light.

Recognizing these exegetical problems, we are left with the problem of how we are to understand and communicate the concepts of exclusivity and permanence. Assuming the most severe exegesis of the gospels, it remains clear that from our later Hebraic heritage and from what the writers of the New Testament recorded, marriage was assumed and mandated to be both exclusive and permanent. For those who chose to marry, these conditions were taken to be a part of the created order. Again, we recall that while the couple may be the ministers of the marriage rite and the priest the witness and proclaimer of blessing, it is God who joins man and woman in marriage.

God, in the person of his son, became the most dramatic and profound example of one who loves. According to both scripture and tradition, this same God is involved with, cares for and loves those who marry. Those who marry in the context of the body of Christian believers and seek to keep this loving God involved in their marriage may live in the hope of an exclusive and lifelong relationship.

There are, in addition, simple and practical reasons for these qualities of exclusivity and permanence. If the number of marriages ending in divorce which involve a secondary relationship for either the husband or the wife (or both) is any indication, the maintenance of multiple concurrent man-woman relationships is simply too difficult. There are too many feelings and other factors to be juggled at one time to carry it off. The king in Margaret Landon's *Anna and the King of Siam* maintained that a man is like a honeybee, going from flower to flower to flower. We do not speak of flowers but of people who have needs such as the feeling of being valued and the sense of making what we have come to know as commitment. The plain fact is that it is difficult enough to love one person with all one has without complicating the matter by engaging in additional relationships. Recognizing that there is a chicken-and-egg problem here as to whether marital problems or extra-marital relationships come first, in the tradition of Christian marriage, permanence and exclusivity are to be valued as the most fulfilling patterns for the married state.

We must be careful not to assume that the basic challenge to exclusive and permanent marriage is secondary relationships. There are as many reasons for marital breakdown as there are people who are married; for the union of two unique creations of God into one does not negate the uniqueness of each.

No basic tenet of the faith is so directly applicable to the marital-love relationship as redemption. As Christians we profess that by the sacrifice once made by Jesus Christ, son of God, upon the cross, the world was redeemed from both sin and death for those who would believe in him and follow in his path. The only way that redemption, the buying back from sin and death, makes any sense to me is to believe that the realities which are redeemed through Christ are the relationships of which each of us is a part. Such relationships are to be identified in the three dimensions outlined in the Summary of the Law:

> Our Lord Jesus said: Hear O Israel, The Lord Our God is One Lord and thou shalt love the Lord thy God with all thy heart, and with all thy soul, and with all thy mind, and with all thy strength. This is the first commandment. And the second is like, namely this: Thou shalt love thy neighbor

as thyself. There is none other commandment greater than these.

—*Mark 12: 29–31.*

Surely the world which is redeemed is not simply the rocks and hills, the birds of the air and the fish of the sea, or even that most magnificent creation of God, humanity. Rather, the redeemed realities are the constituent elements of our life experience, namely, our personal relationships with God, our relationships with the rest of God's creation and, finally, our relationships with ourselves. The three dimensions are vertical (with God), horizontal (with the whole of his creation) and internal (with ourselves—also God's creation).

All three dimensions are integral to what God requires of each of us in response to his love. If I am at odds with myself, I am prevented from loving God and my neighbor as well as I might. If I am at odds with my neighbor, I am prevented from celebrating fully my relationship with myself and from realizing the total potential of my love of God and his love of me. How can I love him while I am at war with what he has created with love, in love? And, most certainly, if I am out of love with God, how can I love myself or my neighbor? God, neighbor, self: these shall we love—concurrently. My closest neighbor is the woman to whom I am married, the person who took me and the person whom I took "for better for worse . . . to love and to cherish until we are parted by death." God is concerned about, and loving toward, my own marital relationship and has many times redeemed it, purchasing it back from selfishness, fear, sloth, anger, pomposity, insensitivity and the threats to our common life which have come with illness, neglect, rejection, failure and terror. But always the starting point is knowing Christ to be God, accepting him as God, and trusting him to use his power in love that we may respond by loving God, neighbor and ourselves.

And so we come full circle, for we are back to "Those whom God hath joined. . . ." God is involved in the reality called Christian marriage. To the Christian, God makes no sense outside the body of Christ, the church. Marriage outside the church is a fact. However, as the *Report on Marriage and Divorce in the*

Church states, "The Church at its best is the Community whose eyes have been opened to what is true for all men."[3]

Having come full circle, we must face the question of what we mean by Christian marriage. We who are engaged in this ministry act as Christian ministers, as clergy or laypersons. We do so in the context of the Body of Christ, a dynamic community with Christ as its head. We certainly recognize that many of those whose marriages we consecrate will rarely, if ever, become active in the church. Some will take their vows recognizing God's involvement, committed to the idea of exclusivity and permanence. Some will begin seriously and later drift away from the church and its ideals. Some will fail to meet challenges to their belief-systems and their marriages will fail. Others will maintain a marital relationship which, for all intents and purposes, will appear Christian while having nothing whatever to do with the church. Others will try as hard as they can to remain faithful to their vows and to their commitment to the church, and yet their marriages will fail. There are couples that will drift in and out of the church while struggling to maintain the integrity of their vows. In some marriages, one partner will be more faithful to his or her vows and to the church than the other. The list of possibilities is nearly endless.

Which, then, are the Christian marriages? It would seem that there can be but one answer: Christian marriage—*matrimony*—is a union of persons which begins at the altar and in which both parties maintain a faithful, growing relationship not only with one another but with the gathered body of Christ as well. Christian marriage is marital love in a Christian context from its beginning until the two are parted by death. This is the ideal. Since God is involved, it need not be dismissed as solely idealistic.

What, then, are we as pastors to do about those couples who come to us all starry-eyed and unaware of the demands and resources provided by God through the scripture, tradition, liturgy and cumulative experience of the body of Christian believers? Again, there can be but one answer: We, the Body, communicate by word and deed all in our power to each couple and believe in what we do as we witness, pray and bless, never ceasing to pray for all those to whom we have sought to minister in this way.

One of the most curious facets of any discussion of marriage is the consideration of its sacramental character. There is a popular misconception that the sacraments of the church, whether two or seven in number, are a definitive reality from the beginning of time. It would seem that many Christians have somewhere in their packet of misconceptions the belief that the twelve disciples met in a hitherto unrecorded council shortly after Pentecost with, perhaps, Peter raising the question,

> "Now that we have the power of the holy spirit, how shall we communicate this gift of grace to the world?"

A voice from the opposite side of the circle was heard to say,

> "Let's have sacraments."
> "Great! What's a sacrament?"
> "Why, a sacrament is an outward and visible sign of an inward and spiritual grace."
> "Fair enough. How many shall we have?"
> "Oh, I should think that seven should do it—and it's a good mystical number. We could have baptism, eucharist, penance, confirmation, marriage, holy orders and unction. How's that?"
> "The outward and visible signs can be worked out by a sub-committee."
> "Well done: womb to tomb. Amen."

Of course, the development of the sacramental system has taken place over the whole of Christian history; and discussion on it continues today within ecumenical dialogue groups at all levels and within every branch of Christendom. An approach might be through a more liberal application of the Latin word which traditionally was used to describe the last rites in the Roman Catholic Church, *viaticum.* If we understand all the sacraments as *viaticum,* that is, God (in love) *with you on the way* through life, from birth to death, celebrating the mileposts along the way, it all begins to fall into place. However, the numbers game is a devilish trap. Protestantism (except for the Quakers and Unitarian-Universalists) holds to two, baptism and holy communion, the Roman Catholics list seven, with the Anglicans, as usual, in the middle. From the new Episcopal Catechism:

Q. What are the two great sacraments of the Gospel?
A. The two great sacraments given by Christ to His Church
   are Holy Baptism and the Holy Eucharist.
Q. What other sacramental rites evolved in the Church
   under the guidance of the Holy Spirit?
A. Other sacramental rites which evolved in the Church
   include confirmation, ordination, holy matrimony, reconciliation of a penitent and unction.[4]

The pre-Reformation German Benedictines are said to have listed twenty-eight sacraments! They included such traditional rites as the anointing of a sovereign at coronation and the act of homage and fealty. The principle of *viaticum* was simply extended. To be sure, it might be said that we express ourselves sacramentally all the time in our speech, our writing and our actions one to another. Any activity carried out in the name and spirit of the Trinity is an outward and visible sign of an inward and spiritual grace, if grace is understood as the love of God in action. Without wishing to join the Arians, the sacraments are a function of those who live in the community of faith.

However, it is easy to see how all this can get out of hand. Hence, with marriage and all other activities of Christian persons, the church found it necessary to define more carefully the administration of the sacraments. Throughout the discussion of marriage as a sacrament, one idea and a continuing controversy set this sacrament quite apart from all the others.

St. Paul spoke of marriage as analogous to the relationship between Christ and the church:

Wives, be subject to your husbands as to the Lord; for the man is the head of the woman, just as Christ also is the head of the church. Christ is, indeed, the Savior of the body; but just as the church is subject to Christ, so must women be to their husbands in everything.

Husbands, love your wives, as Christ also loved the church and gave himself up for it, to consecrate it, cleansing it by water and word, so that he might present the church to himself all glorious, with no stain or wrinkle or anything of the sort, but holy and without blemish. In the same way men also are bound to love their wives, as they love their own bodies. In loving his wife a man loves himself. For no one ever hated his body: on the contrary, he provides and cares for it; and that is how Christ treats the church, because it is his body, of which we are living parts. Thus it is that (in the words of Scripture) 'a man shall leave his father and mother and shall be joined to his wife, and the two shall become one flesh.' It is a great truth that is hidden here. I for my part refer it to Christ and to the church, but it applies also individually: each of you must love his wife as his very self; and the woman must see to it that she pays her husband all respect.

Ephesians 5: 22–33.

As has been noted, marriage as we know it was reserved for those men who could provide a home and support a wife and family. Paul certainly wrote of marriage as being a graceful state, which leads one to think that it should have been encouraged by the church to a far greater extent than it was, regardless of the economic consideration. It was the Parisian theologian Peter Lombard, who died about 1160, whose theology of marriage predominated (along with that of St. Thomas Aquinas) down to the Reformation. It was he who directly related marriage, in both its consensual and its carnal aspects, to the relationship between Christ and the church. The continued development of this thought gave rise to the idea that the *magnum sacramentum* of Christ and the church is, in effect, diminished or defaced by the failure of any aspect of any marriage between a Christian man and a Christian woman. Such a burdensome implication is not to be found with any other sacrament.

Both Peter Lombard and his near contemporary, Hugh of Saint Victor, held that Christian marriage was constituted by the free consent of the parties to the marriage, thus defining the primary outward and visible sign of the sacrament as the parties' agreement about their present intention (as distinct from the future intention articulated at the time of betrothal) and the secondary, complementary and inwardly fulfilling sign as the act of coitus. It was for this reason that marriage was often referred to as the "double sacrament." So the controversy was begun which reached its peak at the Council of Trent and continues to this day: Is the outward and visible sign the mutual consent regarding present intention or is this sign the consummation of the marriage? With the exception of the eucharist and baptism, no other sacrament has suffered such disputation as has marriage.

A secondary dispute arose over the identification of the "sacramental moment," that is, the moment in time when the sacrament of marriage happened. Was it at the moment of mutual consent, at the nuptial blessing, or in the act of coitus? This question remains unresolved as well.

It is not possible in this work to disentangle all the arguments which have formed the tradition of the church concerning marriage as a sacrament. What seems clear is that Christian marriage has a sacramental character which we, without doubt, may understand as an essential mystery of the Body of Christ just as we speak of the eucharist in mystical but not magical terms. The seven sacraments were not mandated by our Lord (except for the eucharist and baptism) or created *ex nihilo* by the post-Pentecost community. They are the spirit-filled and effectual expression in and of the Body of Christ.

It takes only a minimal effort to move from the traditional definition of a sacrament to the understanding of marriage, in and of itself, as a sacrament. The marriage of two people to one another becomes to the world an outward and visible sign of the love of God in action. In a Christian marriage in which love of God, love of neighbor and love of self as members of the body of Christ are lived out, grace is shown forth to the world. While this dimension of the sacramental character of marriage is not usually discussed, it has an evangelical force in God's creation.

Great care must be exercised when discussing the sacramental character of marriage. If we are not careful, we find ourselves extending the tradition of the German Benedictines mentioned earlier. We must distinguish between the sacrament of marriage and the potential sacramental character of a marital relationship. This latter understanding of marriage is not in and of itself a sacrament, but a "lesser sacrament," as in the Anglican tradition, or a "sacramental," as in Roman Catholic usage: A sacred object or rite of the church which is like a sacrament but acknowledged to have been instituted by the church. However, marriage itself, as compared with the rite of the solemnization of holy matrimony, may be sacrament-like, the marital relationship being a witness to the reality of God's love and a channel of his grace to the world.

Yet another way to understand this sacramental dynamic in marriage is to recall Paul Tillich's teaching on religious symbols: "The [religious] symbol participates in the reality which is symbolized."[5] Christian marriage involves a variety of symbols and is itself a symbol. A marriage is a Christian community, as two persons are gathered in Christ's name. As a constituent part of the total Body of Christ, a marriage can indeed participate in a reality toward which it points, the kingdom of God.

Coming at the question from yet another angle, the church may be well advised to begin to think of marriage as a vocation. For some unknown reason we have limited the use of this term to those seeking admission to holy orders or to those who would join religious orders. Just as it seems to be an unwritten rule that we should not speak of the vocation of a carpenter, auto mechanic, nurse or banker, the term is rarely, if ever, used of husband or wife. The church seems reasonably at home with the use of the term "vocation" when speaking of those persons who feel called to a rule of life which, in the case of celibate clergy or religious, calls for a commitment not to marry. In the non-Roman Catholic churches, one may be called (*vocatio*) to ordained ministry as a married person. Saint Paul wrote that one could marry if one felt that it was necessary, but he clearly implied that the unmarried state left one freer to serve God as need arose. In the service of the church, the tradition is well established that one may indeed make his or her offering as a single person with impunity. For those who do not seek ordination, the religious life or some recognized lay ministry, why do we assume that marriage is better than the celibate life? The church prides itself on the manner and extent to which it resists the stated or implied values and social pressures of the world. Why is this not also the case with this supremely important decision?

I grew up in a religious tradition in which a call to the ordained ministry was understood to involve the vision of the Lord at the foot of one's bed at 3 a.m. saying, "Come, follow me." It was not until I was an undergraduate that an Episcopal priest asked me the simple question, "O.K., Mitman, what may you do with your life?" I responded with a recitation of the jobs I thought myself capable of doing, from the practice of medicine to hotel management and house painting. He, in turn, responded that I had not, in fact, heard his question. He was asking me what I *may* do with my life. Suddenly, the memory of my mother's lectures on the difference between "can" and "may" came to mind; and I realized that he was asking me what I had the permission of God to do with my life: What was my vocation? What was my calling to serve? Cannot the pastor apply the same question to those seeking to be married?

Vocation to me begins with the knowledge of myself as God gives me that knowledge—of my feelings, of my intuition, and of my intellect. Proceeding from this knowledge is the understanding of what I can be as a beloved child of God. As God informs my person, I am called to apply this knowledge and understanding to what he offers as a context in which I may make an offering that is acceptable in his sight. Cannot, should not, Christian marriage be seen in the same way?

An interesting counterpoint to this concept of marriage as a vocation is seen in the fact that there are but two steps, if you will, in marriage: The first is betrothal or engagement and the second is the commencement of marriage itself. All this can happen in a remarkably short period of time, a month or even less. In the case of vows taken in ordination or in religious orders, the process is very long and involved. An Episcopalian seeking ordination in the United States must have the sponsorship of a priest of the church and a parish vestry, pass a review by a Diocesan Commission on Ministry three times, stand for two psychological examinations, have his academic record reviewed, receive the approval of a bishop two or three times, attend a seminary for three or perhaps four years where his life and work are evaluated by the faculty and pass the General Ordination Examination, all prior to kneeling before a bishop to be ordained. The minimum time involved is five years and it may take four times that long. In religious orders, one is first a probationer, then a novice, then a junior professed and finally after years of testing one's vocation one takes one's life vows; and even so many men and women leave their orders after taking their life vows.

If we come to understand marriage as a vocation, as I believe we should, then we must face the problem of how such a vocation may be tested. We face the immediate difficulty of the fact that testing the marriage vocation by "living in," as one might test the ministry as a vocation by joining a convent or seminary, would be considered living in sin. In and of itself, such a trial marriage approach probably would not work anyway. Only recently have studies been published which indicate that there is a higher incidence of divorce among couples in which the partners have lived together before marriage than among those who have not. (More on this in Chapter 3.) Cohabitation is not the answer. Testing of vocation in the larger context of the body of Christ, that is, with better informed and more conscientiously applied premarital counseling, begins to approximate the testing of the marriage vocation.

To continue the investigation of the vocational character of marriage, it is interesting to compare the marriage vows with the promises made by an ordinand in the Consecration of a Priest.

> "In the Name of God, I, N., take you, N., to be my wife [husband], to have and to hold from this day forward, for better for worse, for richer for poorer, in sickness and in health, to love and to cherish, until we are parted by death. This is my solemn vow." [6]
> "My *brother,* do you believe that you are truly called by God and His Church to this priesthood?"
> Answer: "I believe I am so called." [7]

The former is an exclusive life vow, while the latter is a qualified understanding. How can it be that the church lays a much heavier burden upon anyone who marries than upon an ordinand, especially when one considers the vast difference in screening and preparation?

In the light of all this, to advocate trial marriages is wrong both for theological and practical reasons. What is the way out of the dilemma? The answer seems quite clear: The church must provide better premarital counseling. We, as the Body, must also enrich the lives of those who are married and provide programs for marriage enrichment as well as other programs for specific concerns such as parenting.

In recent years, secular authors on marriage have written a great deal on the concept of the marriage contract. These authors, from Jessie Bernard in *The Future of Marriage*[8] to George and Nena O'Neill in *Open Marriage,*[9] propose that each couple, whether contemplating marriage or not, work out a contract suited to the personality, desires and abilities of each partner. Such a contract would remain operative for a specific period of time after which it would be re-negotiated, taking into account the various changes in the person and the relationship. Exclusivity and the involvement of God may be part of the contract while a commitment to permanence is not.

The church from time to time has used this term "contract" in its discussion of marriage. However, because such contracts as described above are inconsistent with the vows taken in Christian marriage, the idea is only marginally acceptable to Christian theologians. In addition, a contract as a legal device is fundamentally inconsistent with the Christian understanding of Christ as the one who came to fulfil the law, not to extend it further. The church has moved increasingly in the direction of understanding marriage as a covenant. *The Book of Common Prayer* states:

> O God, you have so consecrated the covenant of marriage that in it is represented the spiritual unity between Christ and his Church . . .[10]

In the context of marriage, the idea of covenant is vastly superior to that of a contract with its clear implications of legalism. However, there are problems inherent in thinking of marriage as a covenant when one considers the historical and theological roots of the concept. The historic covenant between God and his people is central to the theology of the Old Testament. Some scholars hold that the original bond or agreement involved little more than the pagan practice of Israel offering sacrifices as dues in return for the help of God in time of war. It was the prophets who introduced personal and community righteousness as man's part in the covenant in response to God's continued faithfulness to his people. Jeremiah (31: 31 ff.) looked forward to an ethical covenant as the basis of a new relationship with God the father.[11] However, the problem raised by the Old Testament interpretation of covenant when applied to marriage is that, in its application, it carries a clear implication of one-sidedness, at least as initiated by only one party. In the Old Testament it was God who offered and Israel who responded: "And God said to Moses ... 'I will take you as my people and I will be your God.'" Exodus 6: 2a, 7. In marriage, there must be mutuality. The fact that God remained faithful in the face of the unfaithfulness of his chosen people is insufficient to erase the fact that the covenant was initiated by only one of the two parties.

The fulfillment of the covenant in Christ, or the possibility of making it functional, that is, no longer solely dependent on the faithfulness of man, does not resolve the problem. The analogy of God's (Christ's) relationship with those whom he has called to the relationship of the groom with the bride remains inconsistent with the ideal of mutuality. After all, the marriage vows—expressions of one's commitment of one's self to the other—are identical in every respect.

In considering marriage, the Judeo-Christian tradition has led us from the concepts of the covenants, old and new, to that of the contract, and back once again to those of the covenants. Throughout this discussion, the language, the thought forms, and the analogies all prove inadequate to the task of providing us with a consistent, coherent, easily-transmitted theology of marriage. We can say that marriage is a little like this and a little like the other but not completely like anything at all. And yet, these same words, thought forms and analogies are all we have to work with. The harder we wrestle with the scriptures, the meaning of the body of Christ, the history of marriage in the Christian tradition, the sacramental character of the marital relationship and the concepts of vocation, contract and covenant, the more we are led inexorably into the *mysterium*.

As always we are called upon to proceed on faith, in the faith, knowing only that God is involved in a loving way; but because he is involved in a loving way, Christian marriage is possible.

We now move from the lofty heights of theology and history to the specific task of preparing persons for what is both implicitly and explicitly understood to be the most important single relationship to which human beings are a party.

:2:

The Initial Interview

The first interview with a couple is critical. It is here in the first meeting that the pastor begins to establish his or her own credibility and thereby begins to establish the all-important trust relationship with the couple, the kind of relationship without which no one concerned can offer, hear or be understood.

The starting point of establishing this credibility is for the pastor to be absolutely clear that he assumes the role of premarital conselor with the utmost seriousness. If we say in the liturgy that marriage should "not be entered into unadvisedly or lightly, but reverently, deliberately and in accordance with the purposes for which it was instituted by God,"[1] one can hardly expect those being married to take their vows seriously if the clergy do not communicate the same or even a greater degree of concern about preparation for marriage.

The couple must be impressed by the pastor's belief in Christian marriage and in his competence to speak of the theological, philosophical and practical facets of a marital-love relationship and by his willingness, indeed, his eagerness to commit considerable time, energy and the whole of his experience to making the proposed union loving, gracious, supportive, honest and a context for individual and collective growth. Such a counselor must be prepared to make his position clearly and unequivocally known and must not fear the consequences of being honest with these children of God entrusted to his care. A forthright statement of the pastor's pledge to offer and respond honestly is essential. Only then can those to be married be expected to respond in kind.

The pastor must take nothing for granted. He cannot assume any degree of understanding or sophistication in any facet of a marital-love relationship. It is manifestly clear that as individuals, each of us is more experienced or mature in some areas than in others. Many of us have blind spots, that is, facets of our life experience which by conditioning, lack of challenge, lack of stimulation or lack of effort have never been examined. Nowhere is it more important to identify these areas of arrested development than in the context of premarital counseling.

One should not assume that because one has been married previously (whether widowed or divorced), one's experience of marriage is sufficient to prepare one for marriage to yet another person. In fact, a case may be made for requiring two people who were once married to each other and now seek remarriage, to contract that they will pass through the entire process of premarital counseling again. It is frequently true that a person who has been widowed or divorced tends to marry a person who bears a strong resemblance to his or her former spouse regardless of the quality of the previous marriage. This principle is entirely consistent with the idea that people often choose to marry those who are very much like their parents. While a man may dislike his mother intensely, she does provide a model for marriage with which he has become familiar. He has learned to cope, no matter how unpleasantly, with a certain type of woman. A similar principle can operate in remarriage after the death of a spouse or after divorce. My own rule is that whatever a person's or a couple's marital experience, the same rules and commitments on my part and theirs must apply. I recall one couple that I had in marriage counseling for over a year asking me to "remarry" them. They had come to me judging that their marriage had died and after counseling decided to remarry one another. Before I consented to celebrate what amounted to a renewal of their vows and in spite of the many hours I had spent talking with them about themselves and their marriage, I insisted on their committing themselves to a full program of premarital counseling. They happily agreed. The same stipulation should prevail no matter what age the couple may be. Age and maturity are not synonymous, nor does age necessarily imply experience in human relationships.

On the premise that nothing whatever—issues, questions, reflections—should be taken for granted in preparing a couple for marriage, the pastor will find himself asking questions which should go without asking and raising issues which should go without raising. He must therefore begin with a straightforward statement to the couple that all he asks of and shares with the couple should go without asking and/or saying. The cumulative experience of the church and society dictates that all concerned suffer the possibility of looking and sounding a bit foolish. It must be made clear to each prospective bride and groom that this statement is standard operating procedure with every couple in order that there be no suggestion that they are being singled out as having peculiar deficiencies. For example, it may or may not be foolish to raise the issue of family finances with a couple, one of whom may be a certified public accountant. The bride may be a CPA, but the groom may assume that he will keep the family accounts. In like manner, to assume that a theological student about to become a spouse understands the nature of Christian marriage, the quality of God's love or what is meant by the sacramental character of marriage may result in the failure to raise the most important issues. The pastor must be prepared to appear at best, naive and at worst, stupid.

Enter the concept of the contract (not to be confused with *contract* as discussed in Chapter I). Once the pastor, in the name of the Body of Christ, has established the fact that he will be taking the process seriously, he may legitimately demand of the couple that a minimum of four hours be set aside for conversation on the proposed marriage. The pattern which I have found most effective is to contract to meet one hour with the couple and one hour each with the bride and groom individually, concluding with a one-hour open-ended session, again with the couple. The first session in such a pattern of conferences may provide an opportunity for getting to know one another, establishing the contract, and raising the most fundamental issues for preliminary discussion. The second and third sessions, the individual interviews, may then be used for raising questions and issues in a context in which the bride and groom may speak their own minds and in which they may raise their own questions regarding themselves, their proposed spouse, relationships with future in-laws and the like. Some pastors schedule individual interviews if they feel that there is a particular problem to be discussed, but few schedule these sessions as a matter of course. I am convinced that the need for such conferences is imperative, as inevitably issues and feelings surface which would be very difficult or impossible to address with the other partner present. How else can the pastor hope to appreciate clearly the individual perceptions and fears of each partner and to compare his or her responses to those of the proposed spouse?

If possible, it is best to schedule the individual interviews back-to-back for two reasons. First of all, it helps to put both the bride and the groom at ease, as the one who is seen second may experience great anxiety wondering, "What's going on in there? What is the pastor going to ask? What has he (she) said about me?" There is bound to be some anxiety if the couple takes the process seriously. Therefore, to help alleviate as much anxiety as possible, schedule the individual interviews as closely together as possible. The second reason is that such an arrangement gives the pastor the opportunity to compare most effectively any glaring discrepancies in points of view or understanding between the bride and the groom. Insights gained in this way may then be shared with the couple in the final session.

The fourth and final session provides both a time for the pastor and the couple to reflect on what they have shared in the previous interviews and for the pastor to share with them what he perceives as crucial to a loving and creative marital-love relationship.

Just as a clergyman is present at a marriage ceremony for two reasons, that is, as a witness for the state and as the one who blesses the union in the name of the Holy Trinity, so is the pastor's role in marriage preparation twofold. First, the pastor's role is to guide each party in the articulation of personal feelings and perceptions regarding every facet of a loving and creative marital relationship for his or her own hearing and that of the partner. Second, the pastor acts as a sounding board for the two engaged people, assisting them in the clarification of their ideas while sharing with them his own understanding of Christian marriage, reflecting on problems which may arise and offering advice and counsel on how problems may be resolved in the most loving and creative manner.

Careful attention should be given to the context and arrangements for the sessions. The place chosen should provide a relaxed, professional and confidential atmosphere. Therefore, an office or study in which the conversations may proceed without interruption or fear of being overheard is essential. The counselor should sit with the couple, not barricade himself behind a desk. It is helpful to encourage the counselees to choose their own seats and to note whether they sit together on a sofa or on separate chairs. Do they sit closely together? Do they hold hands constantly or occasionally? Do they manage to maintain some physical contact or do they seem to avoid one another's body and eyes? Note should be made of the tone of the conversation. How do they treat one another from the moment they arrive? What about their sense of humor—an indispensable ingredient in any human relationship?

While the first three sessions should be programmed to last about an hour, sufficient flexibility in scheduling should be maintained in order for additional time to be taken with issues which may turn out to be of extraordinary importance to the couple.

Time, honesty and openness are the terms of the contract. This is the point at which the couple may choose not to undertake the program. Such a decision is clearly their prerogative. Quite obviously not everyone would be open to such an approach. There may be logistical problems in scheduling the interviews. However, rarely are such problems of sufficient import to deter those who are serious about entering into Christian marriage. Offering such a contract, witnessing to the seriousness with which the church views marriage, and challenging the couple to respond begin the process properly or send the "church-shoppers" on their way. The decision is clearly theirs.

:3:

The Opening Session: Where to Begin

I t is the practice of many clergy to begin with the liturgy itself, using the Order of Service as the primary teaching device. The difficulty with such an approach is that it assumes
that both bride and groom are mature in their faith and that
there is a common ground on which to begin. In fact, in present
society, most people seen by clergy before marriage have not
matured in their spirituality and theological knowledge as much
as they may have in other areas of their life experience. Most are
Sunday school dropouts, if they ever went at all. The norm of
sophistication is likely to be on a sixth-grade level, when they
"graduated" from church at confirmation. We must recall that
the Episcopal church requires that only one party in a marriage
be a baptized Christian. We certainly may not assume that both
parties have been confirmed, that they have taken their confirmation seriously or have continued their growth in the faith of
the risen Christ. To use the Order of Service presumes far too
much knowledge and experience of theology and liturgy to be a
universally acceptable starting point.

It seems far more reasonable to begin with where they are, to
begin, for instance, with the question of why they have decided
to marry at all and why they wish to be married in the church.

If the contract has been drawn as suggested in the previous
chapter, the question of "why marriage in the church" assumes a
different character, since the groundwork will have been laid
concerning at least some of the implications of this decision. This
is a good opportunity for the pastor to plant the seeds of the idea

of christian marriage; for it is to the church as the Body of Christ that the couple has come, not to a personality (the clergyman), or to a building called a church.

Love, especially marital love in a Christian context, is not to be equated with sex. Yet, in our society we must recognize that the idea of sex and sexual activity are very much in the forefront of people's minds. The pastor must accept the responsibility of coping with this fact from the beginning, always wary of the trap of modern gnosticism in which the pastor deals with people on two separate and, perhaps, unrelated levels: the spiritual and the physical. While some pastors may feel uncomfortable with the responsibility of discussing human sexuality, the premarital counselor must face this issue squarely and without embarrassment. It may be helpful to state outright that the matter must be discusssed openly, not because of some personal perversity on the part of the pastor, but because it is such an important facet of human experience.

Pregnancy

So it is that the pastor immediately must face what may be to the prospective bride and groom a most basic question as to why they have chosen to marry at this time in their lives. It may be answered by the fact that the bride is pregnant. It is self-evident that pregnancy alone, while a most serious matter, is an insufficient reason to marry. If pregnancy is the sole reason for marriage, the marital relationship begins under an extraordinary pressure. In such circumstances, the role of the parents in the decision to marry must be made absolutely clear. If the parents of the bride or groom have forced the marriage, it has little chance of success. If the parents are moved by shame and embarrassment, by societal pressure, by the idea that marriage is the only solution to a problem situation or by the idea that "the child must have a father," then the parents of the bride or groom may well offer a better home for the baby than that created by the natural parents. Six options exist in this situation: marriage, the parents of the bride or groom raising the child, the mother as a single woman raising her child, the father as a single man raising his child, putting the child up for adoption or abortion.

An unwanted pregnancy is, under the best of circumstances, a physical, emotional, psychological and, for some, a moral shock. An unmarried, pregnant woman with her intended husband in a pastor's study may well be a traumatic situation. It is quite legitimate to raise the question of whether or not it is in any way possible for the couple to come to a valid decision under such circumstances. The classic advice to a person who is newly widowed is that because he or she has been so traumatized by the event of the death of the spouse, making any immediate life decisions should be avoided. In such cases, remarriage, moving into a new environment or any other radical change in life-style should be postponed for a least a full year. The idea is that the person is so upset, so out of touch with who and what he or she is in this new state that he or she is quite incapable of making valid decisions. Would the same not hold true with a pregnant bride? And yet from the first time the pastor is likely to see the couple, nature dictates only a maximum of seven and a half months to "legitimize" the child and barely three months in which to sort out the whole situation, arrange for the wedding, the home and the like before the woman begins to "show." In the case of grief following the death of a spouse, the pain, anguish and anxiety diminish with time. In the case of an unplanned or unwanted pregnancy, these feelings often increase with time. How can a valid decision be made by any unwed mother and her fiancé? However it remains that a decision must be made, and the pastor is probably the only person who can draw together all the facts and feelings for the future parents to examine in order that their decision may be as informed as possible.

In addition to external pressures, what of the dynamics between this man and woman? Does the groom understand and accept his responsibility in the situation or is he wondering if he, in fact, fathered the child? He may question whether the woman got pregnant on purpose. In this age of easily obtainable contraceptives, this question comes to mind much more readily than in years past. Since the advent of the contraceptive pill, the responsibility for preventing pregnancy has devolved increasingly upon the woman. If any of these questions are on the man's mind, the starting point of the marital relationship will be one of coercion, suspicion and hostility rather than love and trust. The groom may be so angry at himself that he may well be incapable of loving his bride through, or in spite of, his self-directed anger. Concurrently, the bride may well be wondering whether she has trapped this man and may be in great fear that she will find life with him a continuing trauma. What of the feelings of guilt? It can be postulated that any couple entering a pastor's study cannot be blind to the fact that the church does not encourage pregnancy before marriage! If guilt or societal pressures from parents and others are the primary motivating factors in the marriage, all concerned must understand that marriage is not a penance for a sin confessed, although one may think so from what has often been the practice of the church. If the pastor uncovers at any point in the interviews that it is guilt and not holy matrimony with which he is dealing, it would be far more helpful to shift the counseling to that of the sacrament of reconciliation (penance) where it belongs. Holy matrimony may follow confession and absolution; rarely it seems is the reverse true when the bride walks up the aisle four or five months pregnant.

This is not to say that pregnancy should preclude marriage. It does, however, complicate matters considerably, giving the pastor a complex of dynamics through which to guide the couple as the sessions proceed. The pastor and the couple go on with the program regardless of the issue of pregnancy for the basic issue remains: Can these two people love, honor and accept one another in the context of the institution we know as Christian marriage?

Why Him? Why Her?

Assuming pregnancy is not an issue and keeping in mind the importance of the need for the couple to articulate their own feelings and perceptions, we come to the question, "Why do you want to marry him (her)?" So fundamental is this question that it should be raised in the opening session. With this and all other questions, the responses made by each in turn should be noted by the pastor for future reference. This is particularly true if undercurrents of doubt or uncertainty are voiced by the respondents or if the pastor is troubled for any reason by the responses. This is the starting point of personal expression for the couple. Keeping in mind that this may be the first and only time that each has articulated his or her reasons for this decision in the presence of the future spouse, the verbal and non-verbal response of the other should be carefully noted. This is a very personal question to which no stock response can be anticipated. Responses range from the very vague and unexciting to the most moving expressions for which one could possibly hope. The profundity of such responses has little if anything to do with educational or social background. After hearing both responses, it is appropriate to put the question of the compatibility of ideas just expressed. Just as the pastor should not be reluctant to tactfully question superficial, selfish or grossly inadequate responses, he must also be prepared to reinforce particularly hopeful language such as "offering," "she [he] completes me," "acceptance," "sacrifice," "freedom in union," "respect," "wholeness" or above all, "love."

Love

If love of one another is expressed as a reason for the decision to marry, the meaning each partner assumes for it must be pursued. If the word is not used, each partner must understand why.

"What do you mean by love?" Or "You didn't mention love; why do you think that is?" We can certainly say that there is no final definition of love. We all have our own definition, or we should have our own definition, for the word. Since the dawn of time, theologians, poets, philosophers and, in more recent years, psychiatrists have been struggling with the question of the meaning of love. On close examination, their responses are found inadequate to the question. From St. Paul's poem on love in I Corinthians 13 to the struggle with *eros* and *agape* in the church in the first century, to the synthesis offered by Aquinas in the thirteenth century (*caritas*), to C. S. Lewis' *The Four Loves*, the beautifully troublesome character of the question is reflected within Christendom.

Elizabeth Barrett Browning's famous sonnet, "How do I love thee, let me count the ways ..." is a beautifully romantic expression of the occasions in which love is expressed but little is offered beyond the romantic element. Harry Stack Sullivan offers a very useful definition: "When the satisfaction or the security of another person becomes as significant to one as one's own satisfaction or security, then the state of love exists."[1] This definition serves to separate romance and love. However, it fails when compared with the traditional criteria for Christian marital love. My own definition is that love is "the free act of taking on the ambiguity, the total being of another forever." My definition would fail the same test. Neither definition mentions that God is involved in the love relationship. Both definitions are totally lacking in exclusivity as both may apply to one's love for a potential partner, a parent, a child or a pet as well as for an intended spouse. Neither precludes concurrent love relationships with other people, beings or objects. The third characteristic of Christian marriage, permanence, is not to be found in the Sullivan definition, as the satisfaction and security of yet another person may intrude at any time; one would have to choose between loves. My own definition fails in precisely the same way. And what of mutuality? Both definitions are unilateral decisions without the slightest hint of involving a shared or a mutually agreed upon decision.

Lederer and Jackson in *The Mirages of Marriage* take the position that the vows exchanged at the altar in the Christian tradition are impossible and unfair, largely due to the changes through which we pass as we grow older (a reality to be discussed later).[2] However, their analysis of romance and love is most helpful and commendable.[3] While no answer seems to suffice, the understanding each partner in marriage has of the other's concept of this ineffable reality called love must be shared with, if not by, the other. Each partner's feelings and understandings with regard to this question as well as with regard to so many other questions must be acceptable to the other partner.

Having introduced the question of the meaning of love, the pastor may well comment briefly on his own thoughts about the meaning of the word and, at the same time, use the occasion as a kind of example of the manner in which the interviews will proceed. This is also a very convenient and important issue on which to inquire if the prospective bride and groom have previously shared their thoughts and if so, in what way. Were these thoughts expressed and received with sensitivity to the partners' capacity to verbalize? If not, why not? How does each person feel about the response of his or her intended marriage partner? In this line of questioning, the pastor may be introducing these persons to one another in a new and dynamic way and in the process witness first-hand how each deals with ideas, emotions, values and, perhaps, conflict.

If it has not come out of the conversation thus far, the pastor should point out that while we may love one another deeply and sincerely, the love we have for one another may in fact not be of such a character and quality as to sustain a creative, purposeful, exclusive and abiding marital-love relationship. We have only to consider our own feelings of love for family, friends and even pets to realize that loving someone cannot be sufficient reason, in and of itself, for entering into a marriage. As Christian persons, each of us is enjoined to "love one another" yet we all cannot marry one another. The tough question is whether the love each has for the other is the kind of love which we would term "marital love."

Need

A second response to the initial question, "Why do you want to marry him (her)?" may be to the effect that "when we are together, I feel whole," "she completes me," "he is everything I am not," or "we are just so complimentary."

The attraction one person feels for another person of the opposite sex may be based on a subconscious factor that Carl Jung identifies as the *anima,* the basically female characteristics repressed in the male psyche, or the *animus,* the basically male characteristics repressed in the female psyche. Developing his theory, Jung made three basic assumptions which are relevant to the work of the premarital counselor. The first is that although one is outwardly a man or a woman, the opposite (*anima*-female or *animus*-male) is present in one's unconscious. Second, there is a drive within each of us toward wholeness or integration of the conscious and unconscious selves. Third, all of us are prone to, if not driven to, project upon others what we are unwilling or unable to recognize in ourselves.

Typically, therefore, the man is drawn to the caring, passive, nurturing characteristics of the woman; while, in like manner, the woman is drawn to the managerial, aggressive strength of a man. Each is drawn to that which is within the self but which as yet may be uncovered, undiscovered, unclaimed. It might be said that this attraction, identified by many as falling in love, is the vicarious encounter with one's unconscious. Assuming the innate need for wholeness or integration, each is drawn to what he or she needs but can only realize through the other. None of this is meant to demean love or marriage. It is simply a way of seeing and understanding oneself and others.

Assuming the need for integration, three patterns seem to emerge during the course of any marriage. The first is that both the husband and wife mature in the integration of their whole selves, coming to grips and accepting their shadow selves, that is, the content of the unconscious, while sharing the process with one another. The second pattern, which some identify as the process of falling out of love, involves the appropriation of the conscious skills and life patterns of the spouse. Once those outward and visible talents have been assimilated, the man or woman simply has no need for the other; and there remains no need or reason to remain married. The third pattern involves projection. In courtship and the early years of marriage, many men and women who cannot accept their own goodness project it on their spouse. Once such characteristics have been totally projected, one or the other may think or say, "You're simply not the person I married!" This is consistently the beginning of the breakdown of the marital union.

The seeking of the good, then, is the first pattern, the integration of both wife and husband in concert with one another. If both are whole persons, respecting and genuinely caring for one another, they can encounter their spouse at any point and take joy in one another and in their relationship, even in the greatest adversity.[4]

How may these insights be integrated into the premarital counseling process? Some clergy have taken the lead of industry and require couples to take Myers-Briggs Indicator Test. This instrument is used extensively in industry to test compatibility in management staffing. The intention of this test, which takes no more than thirty minutes to administer, is to determine how people perceive, how they judge and how they act on their perceptions. The test evaluates the person taking it in terms of extraversion-introversion, sensing-intuition, thinking-feeling and judgment-perception. This is a very helpful tool but requires training in interpretation, time in administration and the cost of purchasing the test. For further information, write the AMSA Foundation, 1441 N.W. 6th Street, Suite B 400, Gainesville, Florida 32601.

Aside from the actual administration of the Myers-Briggs Indicator Test, a general discussion of the theory behind it may be very fruitful with some couples. This is particularly true with couples in which one or both parties have been divorced. It is axiomatic that divorced persons tend to marry the same type of person as that from whom they have been divorced. It follows that never having successfully integrated their own persons, they persist in the patterns of interpersonal relationships established in their first marriage. In addition, these persons are particularly vulnerable because they have practiced escape from marriage once through divorce and are less strongly motivated to endure whatever hardships a second marriage may bring. Finally, due to the position the church has taken on divorce and remarriage after divorce, people who have been divorced are the least likely to receive counseling from pastors before they remarry.

Sexuality

During the general discussion with the couple, as previously suggested, young people rarely anticipate any affirmative approach to the subject of sexuality by the pastor. Where the church and sexuality are concerned, most people coming to be married today only recall the giggles in Sunday school when the subject was approached; and the pastor is usually assumed to hold strict or distorted Pauline views regarding human sexuality. The couple is bound to be anxious about what the pastor might ask concerning their sexual experience, with each other, with other partners or, as we shall see, with themselves (masturbation). It seems only fair at this point to begin to put them at ease with regard to the discussion of sexuality by approaching the question of their sexual relationship near the close of the first session. It is by no means impertinent and is in fact necessary for the success of the whole enterprise to ask, straight out, whether the couple has had intercourse with one another. If the question is put directly with the expectation of a simple "yes" or "no" answer and without a pejorative tone on the part of the pastor, the counselees may be greatly relieved to have the matter out in the open and to realize that their responses, if affirmative, will not be met with a devastating quotation from St. Paul or, if negative, will not evoke an air of incredulity from the pastor. For all the sexual liberation of our generation, it must not be assumed that every person coming to be married is sexually experienced with his or her proposed spouse or with others. It can be as much of an anxiety or embarrassment for the person to admit to no sexual experience or limited sexual experience as it may be for others to share with a pastor their wide experience. The question of sexual experience at this juncture is best limited to that which they have experienced with one another. Past experiences with other partners must initially be raised in the context of the individual interviews. As did our Lord with the woman at the well, we must accept people where they are and not where we are, where we might be or where we hope they might be. Where the couple and the pastor go from this point in the body of Christ is what matters.

Cohabitation

The concomitant question for those who respond affirmatively to the question of whether they have had intercourse with one another is whether they are living together. In the course of the conversation, it may have already been mentioned or the answer to this question may have been assumed by the pastor when the initial information forms were filled out; the same address and telephone number for both bride or groom is a bit of a hint.

While cohabitation is a fairly recently recognized phenomenon in our society, although it has been happening for centuries, since 1976 studies have been done which bear directly on the effectiveness of such arrangements as premarital laboratories. Jeffrey M. Jaques and Karen L. Chason, writing in *The Family Coordinator* (January 1979), the journal of the National Council on Family Relations, state that "pre-marital cohabitation may not provide types of learning experiences that significantly alter—in either a positive or negative direction—an individual's preparation for marriage." Using some of the same studies as well as more recent data, Paul R. Newcomb of Florida State University concluded in the *Journal of Marriage and the Family* (August 1979), published by The National Council on Family Relations, "cohabitation was not a more effective screening device than traditional courtship patterns." Parenthetically, Newcomb also writes that "individuals who have experienced multiple marriages are more likely to cohabitate than nonmarrieds or once-marrieds."

I have heard others cite yet another study which went considerably beyond those of Jaques, Chason and Newcomb by saying that divorce rates among those who have cohabitated for an extended period of time, defined as six months or longer, are actually higher than among the population as a whole. Unfortunately, my search for documentation of this assertion has been to no avail. Nevertheless, in dealing with couples who are living together, it is important to challenge any presuppositions of assurance of marital bliss which they may base upon an experiment in cohabitation.

But why do such attempts at relationship development and testing fail to succeed after a man and a woman have met so many of the challenges that are also involved in marriage and then make their decision to marry? I would suggest three possible reasons for the failure of marriages of people who have first lived together.

The first is that those people who feel the freedom to live together without "papers" or "out of wedlock"—a phrase I find most distasteful with its suggestion of a kind of marital chastity belt—are likely to be the same people who would find it difficult to accommodate themselves to the traditional model of marriage in which an exclusive commitment of mutual fidelity, support and love is made "until we are parted by death." It must be remembered that the relationship between two such persons has begun outside the traditional model and, therefore, the likelihood of adhering to other models of marriage is at the very least tentatively established.

The second reason would have to do with the nature of commitment. Living together, cohabitation, can take many forms, from the most conservative model of quasi-marriage to an arrangement of pure convenience in which there may or may not be any sexual relationship between the couple. The couple may have worked out some sort of contract or their cohabitation may have been an arrangement made on the spur of the moment. In such cases the likelihood of having a "till death do we part" commitment is slim. The crunch comes when such a couple enters the pastor's office and realizes, as they must, that they will be required to stand up before each other, family, friends and God to have their union witnessed and sealed with a blessing in the name of the Trinity. A full discussion of the nature of this new commitment to one another is imperative. Realizing this new dimension, I have counseled two couples who, after living together for an extended period and then making the decision to marry and receiving their premarital instruction, separated completely until after the solemnization of their marriage, thus dramatizing the fact that something (the concept of commitment?) had changed and so must their life style. Those were quietly exciting events for all who understood what had taken place.

Finally, while this may not be an original thought, I am convinced that some people marry after living together in order that they might divorce. The reason is that for many, primarily those who have rather backed into their relationship without a clear and specific beginning of their relationship, there can be no way of concluding the arrangement; hence, marriage and divorce.

The most important role of the pastor in this instance is to debunk the myth of the "trial marriage" as a guarantee of marital bliss. The pastor should lead the counselees into a clearer understanding of what they experienced while living together and of how the commitment to be made in marriage makes them now somehow different as individuals and as a couple.

Families and Role Models

The interview should end on the question of how each party in the marriage gets along with his or her parents and prospective in-laws. This must be raised later in the individual interviews as well. However, it is helpful to note the responses of each person to the mention of the other's parents as well as his or her own while the two people are in one another's presence. On the average, one partner in three will have parents who are divorced and one in four will have parents who have remarried at least once. If divorce of the parent is a factor, it is imperative that it be investigated. The important point to be made is that our parents are our most common role models. They provide images for us, patterns of behavior to follow both as individuals and as married persons. If either of the two counselees is the child of separated or divorced parents, it is appropriate at this point to begin to raise questions about what influence the parents' divorce has had on this person's life and what effect this person perceives the divorce to have on his or her views of the proposed marriage. I recall having heard of one priest who, on learning of the divorce of the parents of either party to a marriage, makes a considerable effort to interview the divorced parents as well as their offspring. His reasoning, as one trained in transactional analysis, is that if there are multiple sets of parents, the "parent tapes," uncontrolled conditioning by the parents in our formative years, may be so confused as to require specific therapy in order that the parents may be understood by the couple and dealt with as individual, adult persons. He requires that all this be sorted out before he will consent to solemnize a marriage. Putting this into practice would be most difficult given the time and resource commitment as well as the problems inherent in our transient society. Nevertheless, the idea is worthy of consideration.

Just as parents provide role models for marriage, the friends, siblings or other peers of the bride or groom often provide the couple with an image of married life which they consciously or subconsciously might seek to emulate. A simple inquiry into this matter is in order, and the matter may be pursued as seems appropriate. The primary question which may be answered by this query is just what the couple feels it wants to look like in marriage.

This and every session should end with the opportunity for the bride and groom to ask their own questions of the pastor or of one another or to reflect on their feelings. Up to this point the session has been controlled largely by the pastor. Turnabout is fair play. It can also be helpful to ask the two people in the privacy of their own homes to reflect on their own degree of honesty up to this point. On a scale of one to ten, how honest has each of us been with one another? On the same scale, how helpful, disturbing, encouraging or depressing has the session been? These are questions to which the two counselees should not be required to respond verbally at this time unless they express a desire to do so. In this way, the pastor can challenge the couple but in a non-threatening manner.

A closing note: Some may ask whether the prospective bride and groom should discuss their responses, thoughts and questions with one another prior to the individual interviews. In my experience, most do not ask the question. What is important is to begin the individual interviews which follow with that very question, "Have you discussed the substance of our last session with one another or with others? If you have, what have you discussed? If you haven't, what were your reasons?" By the time of the individual sessions, one would hope that such discussion would have taken place. The response to this question can be an index of the effectiveness of the approach to marriage preparation outlined in this book. It can also provide the pastor yet another insight into how the couple handles ideas, problems and the whole concept of marriage as being a most important decision, a shared decision.

:4:

The Individual Interviews

After reading the previous chapter, it may well occur to the reader that there are two basic problems with the written format of this design for marriage preparation. First, because this design is dialogical, by definition, the discussions cannot be predetermined. The pastor cannot be assured of clear, sequential responses which can be based upon purely analytical, logical processes. The second problem, closely related to the first, is that it is impossible to separate the issues and questions to be addressed from the content of the responses which come from both the couple and the pastor. To be sure, the text would be neater if I were able to clearly label the issues and questions on the one hand and the discursive material on the other. In premarital counseling, we deal with unique individuals, people who are in a unique relationship one with the other; and the pastor is unique as well. The uniqueness of the characters involved in this enterprise produces variables so numerous that to attempt to organize the material in any more structured way would result in a computer-program approach: A decision-table, look-up format or, if (not) this, then (not) this. The dialogical method does not lend itself to binary codification.

I would not wish to imply that premarital counseling is different in this respect from any other counseling. We simply recall that there are issues and questions and there are responses. The responses raise yet other issues and questions which in turn demand from the counselor all the scholarship, experience, compassion and intuition which is his to share.

The Interviews

It makes no difference whether the bride or the groom is seen first. Leave it to them to decide. The important revelation to the pastor and hence later to the couple is how the decision is made: By fiat of the bride or the groom, by mutual agreement or by external circumstances. Even in this ostensibly insignificant matter, the pastor observes, reflects and, when appropriate, shares with the couple that which may be deemed important.

As has already been suggested, each of the individual interviews should begin by questioning what the couple has shared together since the last session. What matters have they discussed? What has bothered or encouraged them? What was the tone of the discussion: Reflective, argumentative, hostile, excited? How does the bride or the groom feel we are doing with our contract? If there was no discussion between the couple in the interim, why was this the case? Was it logistics, fear, the assumption that they should not talk about it or a quiet joy in sharing the event and the prospect of that which is to come as the conferences continue? Again the importance of these questions is twofold: To offer the pastor an opportunity to observe their responses for present and future reference and to encourage creative communication between the two people at this crucial time in their lives.

Reflections on the previous sessions aside, the purpose of the individual interviews is to begin to paint a portrait of the proposed marriage primarily for the couple and secondarily for the pastor given the resources at hand—the bride, the groom and the experience of the pastor. The aim is to examine the various facets of the relationship in as unprejudicial a way as possible and to begin to project the potential this relationship has in the immediate, intermediate and long-range future.

A caveat on two matters: Two reasonably common circumstances should be kept in mind throughout these individual interviews. The first and more common is whether the proposed marriage is the second (or third) for either or both partners. The second is whether there is any significant age difference between the two partners. In the first instance, care should be taken that the marriage is not precipitous in the sense that the bride or groom may not have dealt sufficiently with the previous marriage and that, whether in the case of death or divorce, the grief process may not have been worked through. In the latter case, in which a disparity of age may exist, both partners must understand all the implications of this fact for the years to come, such as the likelihood of an earlier widowhood and a possible difference in the desire for sexual activity which may occur. As each facet of the proposed marriage is discussed, both of these circumstances and the manner in which each may affect the relationship should be kept in mind.

A good way to begin dealing with new questions and perhaps the most unthreatening starting point is to ask the bride or the groom how they spend their time together. What do they enjoy doing together, what do they discuss and to what depth do they share their inmost feelings and thoughts with one another? How are the decisions made concerning how they should share their time? Do the desires of one tend to dominate, are the desires of one followed on one occasion and those of the other on the next or are plans made by mutual agreement? Are there activities in which one party refuses or politely avoids participation? Why? What separate interests are pursued by each party and how are such activities and time commitments perceived and honored by the other?

While there are ways in which this series of questions may appear innocuous, the alert pastor may observe many qualities, or the lack of many qualities, in the couple being counseled. While one pursues the question of how their shared time is spent, the character of the relationship itself begins to emerge as well as the manner in which decisions are made. Feelings about goals and about the vision each has of the future begin to be revealed. The all-important issue of change in a relationship as the years pass is tentatively approached at this stage as is the issue of individuality in marriage, about which more will be said later.

Communication

The responses also reveal the level and character of communication between the two, the first major issue to be faced in the individual interviews. Two people who cannot share their feelings before marriage must be made aware of the fact that they will find communication just as difficult but even more important after marriage. Should the pastor note that the prospective bride and groom have difficulties sharing feelings, ideas, goals or images of the future, it is imperative that the importance of the quality of such communication be impressed upon the couple. One must realize that communication is a learned skill and not something to be taken for granted.

Communication is a two-way enterprise. One partner may be skilled at self-expression and the other may not comprehend what is being expressed. But the process does not end there. Can each party comprehend and accept the verbal and non-verbal response of the partner to statements he or she has made? For example, a man may wish to begin a family (at worst, "to produce a son and heir") and may communicate this desire to his wife. She, on the other hand, may wish to finish her education or to continue a career or enjoy establishing a home with the freedom which comes with the absence of children. She may feel no vocation to motherhood; she may be burdened with fears of conception, pregnancy, childbirth or the rearing of children. She may not feel that she or her husband is ready for such an undertaking, fearing that the division of responsibility in raising children may be insufficiently established or that one partner may be simply too immature to make this decision at this time. The list may go on and on.

The next step in understanding the process of communication is to study the manner and degree to which the husband can comprehend her reasoning and feelings and, in turn, how he responds. To reverse the situation, the issue of a vasectomy later in life may be very traumatic for the husband. Fear of loss of manhood, fear of the surgery involved and fear of a future situation in which he may once again wish to father children are common responses in a man. He may well understand that these fears must be balanced against the assured freedom to express his love for his spouse sexually without fear of an unplanned or unwanted pregnancy. In such an instance, the husband may be quite able to express his feelings and his wife may understand them. However, can he accept her feelings if she sees the matter as one involving a very straightforward decision to undergo a surgical procedure which may well improve the quality of their lives? And so the dialogue continues and a decision must be made. The degree to which the decision is well-informed and conscientious will depend upon the quality of the communication, the degree to which each is heard, and the extent to which the feelings of each are honored and respected. Once any decision is made, whether great or small, does love continue to grow, does the relationship deepen? These are the most important questions.

Decision-making and Conflict

In order that the question of communication may be taken out of the theoretical realm, it is helpful to investigate just how these two persons manage communication, the decision-making process and conflict. To avoid the situation of the pastor merely lecturing the couple, the pastor may probe into the substance of the last disagreement, argument or fight between them. Once such an event is recalled, the pastor can pursue the details: What was it about; what was it like; how was it resolved; how do each of the parties feel his or her position in the disagreement was received? If the partners in the proposed marriage can cite no interaction which could be described as a disagreement, an argument or a fight, how would they each explain the fact that they are an exception to the rule, given the fact that most human beings do have such experiences? Should the latter be the case, it is important that the couple understand that conflict is quite a natural, indeed, a necessary reality in our lives. Lack of conflict quite often reflects a denial of the natural human emotion of anger. A life, a marriage, spent in denial of this basic response is bound to result in repression or internalization of feelings, denial, unresolved hostility, ulcers and in quite a real sense, the death of the person. Where the death of any part of the person has occurred, the marriage is diminished proportionally as either of those involved are less than what the creator had intended. A test case for communication might be made from an examination of how these two people decided to marry one another. The bride or groom may suggest or recall yet another example of an issue or event which exercised their minds and feelings. The pastor must make it clear that he is neither trying to dredge up old quarrels so that they might be resolved in some new way, nor is he planning to sit in judgment on any situation described. What he must communicate is that while he may find shame or guilt in these persons, they are not to be condemned simply because they experience conflict.[1]

Three books which can be helpful to the pastor are *Church Fights* by Speed Lees, *When I Say No I feel Guilty* by Manuel Smith and *The Intimate Enemy* by George R. Bach and Peter Wyden.[2] Because they tend to strike so close to home, these three works provide a laboratory for dealing with our own feelings as counselors. This is often the most helpful place to start in assisting others to deal with communication, decision-making and conflict.

In this exercise of recalling an incident from the past, the pastor makes note of whether each party in turn uses the same example, how each interprets what happened and why there may be differences in interpretation. In the final interview he must not shrink from offering his reflections, in as unthreatening a manner as possible, on any differences he has noted.

Psychological Facet

A second major question to be raised with men and women proposing marriage is how each would characterize themselves in psychological terms, how each would describe the nature of the interaction of the two types and how each feels about such a combination in marriage. We have all grown up with pithy statements about the type of people who should marry. "Opposites attract" may be true with toy magnets, but it is not a sufficient basis on which to build a marriage. "They go together like two peas in a pod" is cute but the analogy breaks down very quickly; peas are grown for consumption or seed but will rot if proper care is not taken, and so on.

What we are looking for here, what the couple should recognize and find acceptable, is how each person's type of personality interacts with that of the proposed spouse. For instance, how would they characterize themselves in terms of being essentially dominant or submissive? Are there instances in their experience of one another in which one pattern prevails; while at other times, on other issues, the opposite may be the case? Another set of categories which may be helpful for those who can comprehend the matter would be those offered by Carl Jung: Would the parties characterize themselves as primarily rational, intuitive, sensing or feeling types of persons? Or, again, in Jungian terms, how strong is the *anima* (the characteristically female component) in the man and the *animus* (the characteristically male component) in the woman? In each of the individual interviews it is most important for the pastor to ask the counselee to characterize not only himself or herself but also the other party and for the pastor to note carefully the responses and the degree to which they are in agreement.

Here again, there are no right or wrong answers. We cannot state that there is any combination of types that always works. Nor can we say that a healthy, loving, creative marriage between any two particular types is impossible. Again, the function of the pastor is to facilitate articulation in psychological terms of the self-comprehension of each party individually and as a prospective married couple, to facilitate reflection on just how this works out in the practice of the relationship and to offer any helpful reflections on what he hears or sees expressed. In sum, it is the pastor's duty to help each clarify just what he or she is getting into and what each is bringing to the union in order that the character of the relationship may be most clearly understood.

Just as in other areas, the bride or groom may be quite surprised at this line of questioning. Certainly, a sign of danger is to hear and see hostile responses. More than likely such hostility is grounded in discomfort or dis-ease. This may be natural. However, the pastor may find it necessary here or elsewhere to recall the terms of the contract: Time, honesty and openness.

At this point in the interview, it may be helpful to extract an example from the couple's own experience as previously described in order to illustrate the point. Or the pastor may remind them of an ostensibly extraneous issue such as their relationship with their parents or with their prospective in-laws. How does each respond to each set of parents from a psychological standpoint and what has this to do with where they are coming from and how they might be expected to respond to one another in marriage?

For example, suppose invitations were received from both sets of parents for Christmas dinner, that all lived in the same community and that all had the day free. The husband may decide that the two of them will have dinner with his family and his wife may be pleased with his having made the decision. Should the wife have difficulty with her family over the decision, she may place the blame on her husband. Here we see clear indications of a woman who is content, at least for the time being, to be married to a man who takes initiative, makes decisions and organizes their lives. Reversing the situation, the problem or conflict may be resolved by the wife working out a complicated yearly schedule involving a complex of trade-offs between his family, her family, and their own family, between hosting holiday and special-event festivities and accepting the hospitality of others, between Thanksgiving, Christmas, Easter, birthdays, anniversaries and other traditional festive events. In such a resolution, a woman may exhibit extraordinary organizational and management skills, the very skills which are attributed most frequently to the male. How would the husband react to such a circumstance—with rage, gratitude, total passivity, jealousy, or would he seek to participate in the process or offer to assume a similar responsibility at a later time? A third but by no means final alternative would be for the husband, wife or the couple to permit their parents to make the decision for them. What would this indicate about the couple's psychological and emotional maturity? In any circumstance in which the action, lack of action or attitude of one or the other partner results in the diminution of the personhood or sense of self-worth of the other, destruction results. It is the capacity for, or likelihood of, just such destruction which may be anticipated by a discussion of psychological compatibility.

The example given above is not necessarily a hypothetical question. This or a similar situation may already have occurred in their relationship.

Role Definition

A great deal has been written in recent years about role definitions. This issue relates quite directly to psychological patterns of behavior. While much of the research and writing of the women's liberation movement has been summarily dismissed by those who are most threatened by its implications, there is much to be learned from this school of thought. It is manifestly true that our responses are quite often conditioned by the role models presented to us by our grandparents, parents, siblings, the media and our most intimate peers. A man who is not only willing but happy to share in responsibilities of child care, housekeeping or meal preparation may be the brunt of the most cruel and insensitive remarks: "It isn't manly!" Conversely, women in business or manual jobs or those who are primary breadwinners are sometimes subjected to the most unkind questioning of their femininity. Such women are often not considered "ladylike"! And yet, there are male chefs and Roosevelt Greer, the needlepoint aficionado, on the one hand and Katherine Graham of the *Washington Post* and former Congresswoman Barbara Jordan on the other. The most radical models aside, any couple coming to be married nowadays must confront conscientiously and directly how they propose to divide and share their domestic and professional responsibilities. It has been my vocation in recent years to be pastor to academic communities. It is often the pattern in such contexts that the groom or husband is being educated "by the sweat of his frau." Frequently, the wife is working and caring for children at the same time. Traditional roles are in question from the beginning of the relationship. The shock of adjustment comes when the husband has completed his degree and takes a job. What adjustments are then required? Does the woman wish to continue working because she finds it personally fulfilling or will she work out of economic necessity? Does she want to begin a family or continue her professional life? If so, how will the decision be made? Given the culturally-conditioned traditional role models, how will the husband and wife react and what factors will affect their responses? What defines the personhood of each as these changes occur; or are we still talking about his "manhood" or her "womanhood"? In the premarital counseling setting, we may not be able to settle all these issues. However, it is imperative that the subject be raised and the process begun.

In this whole matter of role definition, the pastor must be with both parties as they attempt to project how they will work out their freedom to be themselves, based upon mutually determined and agreed-upon terms, within the context of Christian marriage. The issue becomes one of liberation in the community of the marriage rather than one of "women's liberation" or "men's liberation." This concept is entirely consistent with Christian faith experience taken as a whole, selected passages from St. Paul notwithstanding. We are offered freedom in our relationship with God in Christ through the power of the spirit: "What Christ has done is to set us free, to be free men [persons?]. Stand firm, then, and refuse to be tied to the yoke of slavery again," (Galatians 5: 1) and "Where the Spirit of the Lord is, there is liberty," (II Corinthians 3: 17).

The women's movement is not simply going to go away. It is an appeal for human fulfillment which can be realized in the context of marriage. Because we believe that our Lord came to set us free from the bondage of sin and death, we rejoice in the liberation of those who recognize the liberation of others. The pastor's responsibility is to guide the couple to the threshold of this celebration that individually and together the bride and groom might become all that God intended them to be.

The pastor may well suggest that the couple write out a schedule of duties inside and outside the home and come to some tentative decisions as to who will do what: Cooking, bed-making, cleaning, shopping, lawn and garden maintenance, child care, communication with parents, brothers and sisters (often considered a distasteful task), etc. The opening question may be what does each like to do? The responsibilities which are least attractive to both may then be divided. This may again be urged on the couple as an exercise in communication and decision-making. Each partner may be quite surprised by what responsibilities the other may choose to assume. While this schedule or duty roster should not be mandated by the pastor, it may prove a welcome suggestion. Certainly, the division of responsibilities needs continuous revision as circumstances change within the marriage.

Sexuality: Background

Before the individual sessions proceed much further, it is helpful to raise the issue of sex. From the onset, we would do well to recognize that there are two quite opposing forces, related though they may be, which confront the pastor and the couple. The first is that we are part of a culture which has raised sex, in its most oppressive forms, to the level of our human *raison d'être*. As Americans, we are bombarded with sex and prohibitions about sex from the time we begin to learn and assimilate. The second force which is operative in the minds of the bride or groom facing the pastor is the widely held presupposition that the church is against sex: "If it feels good, it must be bad!" is a common attitude reflecting our Puritan heritage. Because of these conflicting forces, each party to the marriage may bring an understandable measure of anxiety to the discussion of the matter. In order that the subsequent conversation will not be overshadowed by such a cloud of anxiety, it is helpful and thoughtful to raise the issue fairly early in the individual interviews.

Discussion of sexuality, sexual experience and fears or anxieties is imperative given the astonishing naiveté of most people in this area of human experience. A public school course in human sexuality, a *Playboy* column, a *Ladies Home Journal* article or even instruction from parents usually misses the mark mainly because such information is intuitively understood by many brides and grooms to be an incomplete if not a false view of the totality of human sexual expression. Sex education is really not the issue. Who, after all, does not know about stimulation, erection, menstrual cycles and pregnancy? How to place the penis in the vagina and make the appropriate movements is not the question. The issue is first of all just how sexual activity, not limited to intercourse, contributes to the quality of the marital-love relationship. Each party in marriage must question whether or not their physical relationship has a sacramental character about it and whether such a shared experience is an occasion for a most important form of communication. A sexual relationship may run the gamut from being merely an exercise in mutual masturbation to being the celebration of a union of two children of God who are devoted to fulfilling one another in every possible way, "an outward and visible" expression of a love perceived as sacred.

Let us begin by clearing away some of the cobwebs: People should not be made to feel guilty that their sexual expression may be recreational (physical intimacy that is enjoyable for its own sake), procreational (intercourse with the intention or hope of conception, an occasion which may be packed with all sorts of anxieties) or informational (a time of learning to know one another emotionally and physically, a situation in which verbal and non-verbal communication comes into play). The list does not stop here. Intercourse or other sexual intimacy may be an occasion of reconciliation following a disagreement or an out-and-out fight. Offering one's love to one's beloved is a beautiful, wondrous and fulfilling action.

In our culture, intercourse has too often taken the place of intimacy. One may call to mind a legal question, often posed in divorce cases where adultery is an issue: "Were you and . . . [sexually] intimate?" Intercourse is not equal to intimacy. However, without a real sense of intimacy, knowing and being known, "naked and unashamed," sexual relations will soon fail to be satisfying. Intimacy is knowing the personhood of another as compared with knowing about another or simply using another person to satisfy a physical desire or need. Such an idea is entirely consistent with the translation from scripture of the Hebrew word for intercourse, "knowing."

Intimacy may well be achieved without a sexual dimension, an idea most unpopular in our permissive society. For instance, in a pastoral context, clergy and counselors certainly come to know those whom they counsel most intimately just as they, too, are similarly known. The archetypal person of our Lord comes to mind. While the disciples found it very difficult to know Jesus, at least according to St. Mark, Jesus was on the most intimate terms with his followers. He knew them and yet there was no legitimate suggestion of a sexual relationship with the disciples or with the women who followed him. Sexual intercourse can be had. Intimacy is the reality to be celebrated.

Sexuality: In Dialogue

It is all very well to talk about sex on a theoretical plane. The problem comes in precipitating a helpful dialogue about the problems and potential of human sexuality, all with a strong grounding in theology and philosophy. The pastor must clear the first hurdle quickly, straightforwardly and without any pejorative tone in his questions. If the man or woman sitting opposite senses that the pastor is sitting in judgment of the person's sexual experience, no matter what the pastor may actually feel, the bride or groom will be put on the defensive and the pastor cannot be helpful. The pastor must not build walls with his attitude.

With assurance of strict confidentiality, he must pose the question, "What has been your sexual experience with *N.* or with others? Have you had intercourse?"

Here the conversation may take two basic courses depending on the response. The pastor becomes primarily a sounding board if the response is affirmative or primarily a teacher if the response is negative. For obvious reasons there are also differences depending on whether the pastor is talking with the woman or the man.

While intercourse before marriage between persons planning to be married is not yet normative, it is a statistical probability. Assuming for the moment that it is the bride with whom the pastor is talking and that she has responded that she has had intercourse with her fiancé, it is a relief to the woman if the pastor begins probing her feelings about her experience, backing off from the technical questions. "How do you feel about your physical relationship? Is it relaxed or tense—passionate or perfunctory? Is it fulfilling and if so, to whom and in what ways? What does it mean to you? What do you hope to realize in your sexual relationship with *N.?*" Here the pastor offers a variety of questions providing various avenues for response. The point of this line of questioning is to lead the bride, and later the groom, to the more profound understanding of sexual activity outlined above. If her responses are generally negative or questioning, it is imperative that she articulate her concerns, not for the pastor's benefit but for her own. Why does she have these negative feelings? Is she being mistreated? Is intercourse painful or does she fear pregnancy? Does she feel guilty about her experience? If any of the above are true, the pastor must help her and, later, both partners understand why this is the case. If guilt is an issue, some teaching on the sacrament of reconciliation is clearly called for. Marriage is a sufficiently challenging undertaking without beginning with the cumbersome excess baggage of guilt!

The second awkward issue, which follows closely, is whether or not the bride is orgasmic and how often she experiences orgasm. If she does not, how does she feel about the matter? Has she been honest with her fiancé concerning this and how has he responded? What does she think the reason is for her lack of orgasm? Has she consulted a physician; and, if so, what was the response? While it is foolish to assume that consistent or multiple orgasms are necessary to sexual fulfillment, it is likewise necessary to seek out the reasons for the lack of this very natural response in order that the bride may feel even more fulfilled.

The answer may be simply that her clitoris is unexposed, a condition easily remedied by minor surgery. Guilt may be the cause. She may be saying to herself, "I must not enjoy this (yet)." Conditioning by parents or friends may have lowered her reasonable expectations, giving her the notion that sex is to be endured, not enjoyed. Has she experienced orgasm with others or in masturbation? She may simply not be responsive to this particular man, or he may be an unfeeling or inexperienced lover. Yet another possibility is that she may feel herself to be physically unattractive and, therefore, unlovable. We must keep in mind that orgasm in men is readily apparent. This is not so with women. What is the woman to do? Be honest and potentially threaten the self-image of her partner or fake a response and hope that things will change at some point in the future? Though perhaps benevolently intended, to feign orgasm consistently would bring deceit into the relationship. The pot is bound to boil over at some point! Whatever the reason for her limited response, it must be dealt with. Many physicians, obstetricians, gynecologists, psychiatrists and psychologists are particularly skilled in dealing with such sexual dysphoria. It is the pastor's responsibility to guide the woman to someone who can help. While treatment may be expensive, when compared with what we spend to straighten our children's teeth, to repair our automobiles or to stage lavish weddings, it makes sense to seek out all the help available.

A matter which may relate to the above is whether the bride or groom has experienced any sexual trauma in his or her history such as rape, molestation, homosexual or lesbian seduction or rape or incestuous advances. Just as we are required by civil and canon law to inquire into any impediments to marriage, we must recognize that past sexual trauma can easily constitute a physical, psychological or theological impediment to marriage. The question must be simply put; and if the response is affirmative, the pastor must help the couple sort out their feelings regarding the incident(s) or refer them to someone who is skilled in this area.

In the case of homosexuality, it may be quite difficult to identify a therapist who is qualified to deal compassionately and effectively with a person who experiences divided or uncertain sexual preference. But if the bride or groom has been approached, attacked or seduced in what may amount to an isolated incident, the sensitive pastor can usually deal with the matter. Here again guilt may be the predominant question. However, if the person maintained a sustained physical or deep psychological or emotional attachment to a person of the same sex, then specific therapy is imperative in order to determine the possibility of commitment to an exclusively heterosexual marital-love relationship.

The marriage of a person with a divided sexual preference begins on the most unreliable foundation. If therapy is indicated, the pastor must search out qualified therapists in his area. A call to the nearest Dignity or Integrity organizations would probably be the most helpful approach. Each of these groups, the former founded by members of the Roman Catholic Church and the latter by members of the Episcopal Church, are made up of homosexuals who strive to maintain their relationship with God and the Church knowing that they are homosexuals. A listing of local and area chapters of each organization is available by writing

INTEGRITY	DIGNITY International
701 Orange Street	755 Boylston Street,
#6	Room 413
Ft. Valley, GA 31030	Boston, MA 02116

When the pastor calls on such resources he must be very clear that he is not simply in search of a therapist who will give the person a pat on the head or simply assert "gay is best," but one who will be truly helpful in sorting out this most complex problem. In any case, the pastor should certainly make his pastoral skills known and offer whatever help he may.

As for dealing with other trauma listed above, if any such experience has occurred, the pastor must once again look for feelings of guilt, feelings of being dirty or foul and feelings of complicity. Penance, absolution, reconciliation of the person to God, to himself or herself and to the rest of God's creation, particularly the intended spouse and parents, and assurance that he or she is truly and earnestly loved by God and by the proposed spouse is absolutely essential in such cases.

The best advice is not to push the person into a confession of any past sexual deeds and experiences to the other party in the marriage. For some people, there are times when this type of communication can happen naturally and simply. The question should be put as to whether the bride and groom have shared their sexual history with one another to make certain that they have thought through their decision. It is certainly true that such information may be used destructively later in the marriage, particularly at times of extraordinary pressure. Such pressure points will be discussed in Chapter V.

Most clergy are males. Rape is mainly an experience of women: A horrible, traumatic experience. A woman who has been raped may be totally put off by men; or, while she may love one man most profoundly, she may harbor a degree of mistrust and fear which may manifest itself negatively in a great variety of ways. Issues of a negative self-image or fear of intercourse or other physical expressions of love may rest deeply in the subconscious mind of the woman. Women make the best rape counselors. Many communities have established counseling centers to which women can be referred. While there are no firm figures, it is shocking to realize the high incidence of rape in America as well as the fact that a large percentage of cases go unreported. If the proper trust level has been established with the pastor, both women and men may share such experiences for the first time in their lives with a great sense of relief. The issue having been opened, a referral to another therapist is possible.

It is quite surprising to this counselor that in this so-called enlightened age there is so much lingering suspicion, fear and doubt surrounding masturbation. While auto-eroticism is typically more of an issue with women than men, childhood admonitions about pimples and the like too often prevail for both sexes.

Once the pastor realizes the degree to which both men and women are traumatized by the subject if not the practice, it will be realized that for some people bringing the practice out in the open may be a bit awkward but quite welcome. The pastor should pose the following questions as naturally as possible: "How do you feel about masturbation? Do you masturbate? How do you feel about the fact that you do? What place will masturbation have in your sex life after your marriage?" The hypothetical question is more important than the hypothetical answer. What requires affirmation, the Vatican's position to the contrary notwithstanding, is that masturbation is quite a natural activity before marriage as well as after marriage. The point is that auto-eroticism must not take the place of, or impinge upon, the sexual relationship of the couple in marriage. Perhaps more troubling to an individual than the practice of masturbation is the content of the fantasies which accompany such activity. People are most reluctant to share these thoughts with anyone let alone with the clergy or a lay counselor who is identified with the church. We should note that only recently have books been published on what purport to be sexual fantasies. I tend to believe that they are often fantasies of fantasies! Yet, even these fantasies appear to be contributed to the compilers of such books in written form instead of in face-to-face verbal discussion. All the pastor can do at this point in the discussion is suggest that it is helpful to examine our fantasies and that they should be understood as revealing *something* of who and what we are. As always, softly and gently, the pastor offers the couple an opportunity to reflect on their experiences and feelings and to ask questions of themselves or of the pastor.

It is likewise important to inquire into the matter of how the bride and groom feel about their bodily functions. The most obvious stumbling block here is the matter of menstrual periods. If the old wives' tales prevail, the pastor must do his best to dispel any notion of uncleanness during menstruation, the kind of ideas which are unfortunately offered by the authors of the scriptures. Suggestions of "the curse" or the like may be indications of the woman's and, in some instances, the man's reaction and disdain for the human body and its functions. While it is certainly true that there may be physical and psychological discomfort, the menstrual cycle is a most natural and acceptable reality. The groom must be made aware that an extra measure of sensitivity and kindliness may be necessary during this time of the month. The effect of the hormones estrogen and progesterone are different in each woman. However, it may be generally anticipated that her mood may be most agreeable at midcycle, that is, about two weeks before or after her period. Sexual relations including intercourse are perfectly acceptable during the woman's period if such activities are mutually agreed upon. While little is known about the matter, the bride and groom should both understand that men, too, have "periods" of sorts. That is, they may experience times when they may feel more amorous or, conversely, short-tempered than at others, quite exclusive of external stimuli. The woman must be made aware that during such times an extra measure of acceptance and sensitivity is required.

This area of inquiry and reflection might be concluded with a general question as to whether either of the two has any sexual hang-ups or whether either can identify any taboos which may have been handed on by their parents or friends (for example, concerning oral sexual activity). Communication of, and respect for, such feelings is the goal to which the pastor must lead the couple.

Family Planning

Regardless of the dead weight of the assumptions of our society, to assume that it is every couple's vocation or desire to have children is absurd. However, should children be conceived the couple must be prepared to accept, love and nourish them with all they have to offer. It is essential that both individuals understand the various methods of family planning or birth control. Advice on method should be sought from a physician; but two main points must be made by the pastor. First, every method of contraception from the rhythm method or *coitus interruptus* to the pill has its physical, psychological, intellectual, aesthetic or theological drawbacks. Second, the couple should be encouraged to pay another visit to the doctor should one method become obtrusive in their relationship. Even brand names make a difference. I recall a young bride coming to me for counseling who complained of depression, swollen limbs, and one breast growing noticeably larger than the other; and she realized that she was becoming less tolerant of her husband for no apparent reason. I referred her to a gynecologist who simply changed the brand of the contraceptive pill she was taking. While the brands involved had essentially the same formula, there was a difference sufficient to change her hormone balance. In about six weeks time, most of her symptoms disappeared. The message to be communicated is simply not to get locked into one method of birth control because of habit or fear of calling a physician.

Perhaps one of the most important bits of counsel the pastor may offer is to urge in the strongest possible terms that both bride and groom have complete physical examinations before marriage. Blood tests and pap smears are not sufficient! The reason for making this recommendation so strongly is that most young people coming to be married have not had complete physicals in some time and to do so before embarking upon marriage only makes sense. Individuals marrying later in life should be as certain as possible that they are in good health. No matter what the age of the parties, each partner has every right to know the physical condition of the person whom he or she is marrying before the ceremony. I would estimate that in my experience, in one case in four, a serious physical problem was discovered as the result of the physical examination which I had recommended. Newlyweds have quite enough to consider without the added burden of physical ailments.

Of the hundreds of books available on human sexuality, there are only two which I would recommend as resource books for couples preparing for marriage:

Sexual Harmony in Marriage by Oliver M. Butterfield, published by Emerson Press, New York, 1953. This small volume is still in print and is available in paper at $1.25.

Masters and Johnson Explained by Nat Lehrman, published by Playboy Press, New York, 1976. It is hoped that the name of the publisher will not prejudice readers as it is by no means a rehash of the "Playboy philosophy."

The necessity for the pastor to be well informed in the area of human sexuality is clear from the above. What he may recommend to the prospective bride or groom for their own reading will depend upon their needs and their ability to deal with ideas or their intellectual capacity. There is so much to deal with in this area that it is quite impossible to assume that the pastor can treat all the issues in depth. And while he should not be timid in asking questions or offering his reflections on what has been shared, he should feel free to require outside reading when it is deemed appropriate.

Lest the pastor feel a reluctance to delve so deeply into the personal lives of those who come to him to be married, lest he feel rather like an ecclesiastical voyeur, it must be kept in mind that many or most of these issues, questions, anxieties and possibilities for celebration of marriage are not likely to be raised in a helpful and informed context in any other place by any other skilled person before or even after the wedding. This is not a kick for the pastor; it is part of his vocation as a conscientious, Christian counselor.

Economics

Moving from physical to fiscal matters, the pastor inquires into the couple's present and projected financial status. Is there sufficient income to support the marriage? From what sources? If support from either the bride's or groom's family is involved, the question of how this affects such relationships must be posed. Financial assistance from meddling or manipulative parents is certainly to be avoided if at all possible. Can the couple manage if the bride becomes pregnant? If so, how? Who will have primary responsibility for the household accounts? If not already covered in previous discussion, how was the decision made as to who would manage the household finances and how comfortable are both parties with that decision? Has the budget been determined using hard data as opposed to guesses? By whom was the budget designed? Is it acceptable to both bride and groom? It is a common practice in business and government to require consultation and approval for purchases or commitments of funds over a stated amount. A similar arrangement might be helpful in the household as long as both parties agree to the terms of the agreement. If they cannot agree, the matter bears investigation! A suggested budget form is found in Appendix B for the pastor's use. For those pastors who would deem it useful and for those who feel qualified to help with the matter, it may be beneficial to reproduce the form in Appendix B and to ask that the couple fill it out together, making whatever changes in the form they feel appropriate, for a brief review in the final session. It may be helpful to point out what financial counseling services are available in your community or how to begin to look for such services if and when the couple moves to another town or city. Again, household budgeting is a learned skill in which both parties must participate.

Note that the first item of expenses is the budget for the wedding and honeymoon. We do the couple and their families a great service by encouraging them to keep careful track of these expenses. Too often, peer pressure and etiquette books outdistance common sense in budgeting for a wedding and related events. The result is years of debilitating and hostility-provoking debt for the couple and their parents alike.

Spiritual Dimensions

Just as in each of the other facets of the marital-love relationship, it is important that each partner be required to discuss privately with the pastor his or her feelings and intentions regarding God, our Lord and the church. This is a topic which all too often is not discussed by the couple. If anything may be regarded as a taboo subject in this secular age it is the spiritual dimension of personhood, a fear or assumption which is often compounded in marriage. Here the pastor must be quite clear about what he is asking. Religion as an abstract subject may be discussed in the same manner in which one might discuss the relative merits of encouraging or discouraging children to read *Through the Looking Glass*. Personal spirituality, understood as one's relationship to God, Christ and the dynamic gathered community of the faithful, the church, is quite another question.

As opposed to those who profess a strictly "personal" spirituality with the primary emphasis upon one's vertical relationship with God, a relationship which some maintain can be worked out quite apart from community ("Go apart into thy closet and pray"), I gain my greatest strength from the gathered body of Christian fellowship. For me, it is Christian community, the church in its fullness, which provides the context in which saints and sinners gather together to try their faith and works.

For my part, then, the discussion of the spiritual understanding and intentions of persons coming to be married are to be seen against this background. Such a starting point provides a direction in which to go when confronted with the response, "I believe in God but not in organized religion." I too am against organized religion if, as Fr. Vincent Strudwick once said, it is understood as a petrified corpus of indisputable propositions with a specified ritual and behavior. However, I do believe in an all-too-imperfect community of persons sharing the exciting task of seeking the glory, majesty and love of God: The same glory, majesty and love which by the power of the holy spirit may be shared and experienced in the Body of Christ.

What can be done by the pastor in such a limited time to encourage the bride and groom in their journey in faith? Can the pastor even lead them to accept the invitation to the journey? As mentioned earlier, premarital counseling can be a rare and exciting evangelistic event. These people have come to the church to partake of its ministry no matter how naive their expectation might have been at the start. The pastor might begin with a series of questions which offer the couple a variety of avenues of response. One might say, "I realize that we touched on this question very briefly in our first session; however it is important to remember that you have come to the church to be married. How do you see yourself in your relationship to God, the person of the Christ and the church? How would you characterize your spiritual background and growth? Have you discussed this with your fiancé; and, if so, where did you come out? How do you see yourselves relating to such questions in the future, after you are married?"

The imperative which is to be communicated to each partner in the individual interviews is that this is a time in his or her life when it is not simply appropriate but only conscionable to take the question of spirituality seriously. Sunday school religion is an insufficient basis on which to make any decision in this matter. Most people coming to the church to be married will at least admit to a belief in God, whatever that may mean to them. Certainly, both should be required to amplify that statement and to articulate to themselves and to one another, as well as to the pastor, just what they mean. The key question to pursue is that if they profess any belief, has it grown and matured as the years have passed or has it remained static; and, if it has remained static, how long has it thus remained? Do they dismiss the church as a gang of hypocrites; or do they see it as the gathering of sinners in search of redemption and reconciliation with God, self and neighbor? What theological books have they read as adults or are they dependent upon those cursed Hollywood biblical epics for their spiritual stimulation?

In what other area of life would such immature understanding suffice? If the rest of our education ended at the age of discretion as so often happens with one's theological education, our ability to balance a check book, start the lawn mower, write a letter, make our way in the world of work, relate sexually, rear children, etc., would be severely hampered. In any area of human experience or skill other than theology, such a person would be judged to be suffering from a case of arrested development.

While an undergraduate, I used to see a sign on the steps outside a church in Richmond, Virginia, which read, "Enter, Rest, and Pray." It often disappeared only to turn up later in various inappropriate places on the college and university campuses which surrounded the city. The pastor, by his presence and presumed skill, should have succeeded in the first two of the invitations mentioned on the sign; but the third invitation is much more difficult to offer; and to go beyond the third is the most difficult task of all. If the pastor is successful in bringing the couple to the point of assessing their theological maturity, the challenge becomes how to involve them in making an informed and mature decision about their future relationship with God, the Christ and the church. Beware the assertion that the couple will come back to the church "when their children need it." Such people tend to participate in the church for the duration of child-rearing and, after the children are on their way, return to the golf course.

If the couple can be brought to the point of a future commitment to the church, the pastor is then faced with the challenge of asking himself whether there are indeed study and/or support groups within his parish, in addition to Sunday worship, in which he might invite the couple's participation: Groups through which they may continue to mature in the faith in the risen Christ? If there are none, why not?

Several years ago, Harvey Cox of the Harvard Divinity School write a little-heralded but important book called *On Not Leaving It to the Snake*.[3] Written in the years of reaction to the "Death of God" school of theology (I am never quite sure of using "theology" in that context), his thesis is that we fall short of the glory for which God intended us if we, as did Adam and Eve, leave it to the snake, the serpent of Eden, to make our decisions for us, to tempt us or to push us over the edge into a decision which really isn't ours at all. We are created such magnificent creatures. Too often we fail to gather up all our resources, all that we have experienced, all that we are and all that by the grace of God we might be, in order to make our decisions. To refuse to bring the totality of our persons to bear on important decisions is to betray the gift of life itself. In the case of making the decision regarding one's future in the Body of Christ before marriage, it is too often the case that the question is simply not thought out individually or as a couple. What passes for a decision is determined by neglect, immaturity or laziness rather than by informed effort to know what one does believe. John Sisk of Galudette College once said that man's debilitating proclivity is more often sloth than selfishness. I am convinced that the devil wins most battles by default. The pastor simply must not let the couple off the hook in this matter of their spiritual growth. If after conscientious consideration and practice within the body of Christ, first as an engaged couple and later as a married couple, one partner or both should say "no" to God, the Christ and the church, we lament their decision and we keep them in our prayers. Nonetheless, how much better it is if, indeed, it is a decision.

As always, the pastor must weigh the responses of each party, assess the depth to which the two people have shared their thoughts and feelings and share with them any insight he may have regarding problem areas or potential problem areas. Again, this is an area in which few couples have shared their deepest feelings. What will they agree to do together in the area of spiritual growth? If only one chooses to tread this path, how will it affect the marital relationship?

Inter-faith Marriages

We cannot leave this issue without some discussion of the problems and potential of "mixed marriages," that is, marriage between individuals coming from different church or denominational backgrounds. The first observation that should be shared is that many couples use this issue to opt out of the God-Christ-church question altogether. If there are any indications that this is the direction in which the couple is heading, the pastor must bring the couple to the realization that such a course is an excuse and not a decision.

While there may be other answers or approaches, I believe that the very best answer for everyone involved in mixed marriages is to be found in the one, holy, catholic, apostolic and renewed church, that is, the Episcopal Church. But, then, I am hardly a dispassionate observer.

Given the transient nature of our society as well as a myriad other factors, it is a probability that most marriages will be between persons of different religious traditions. The pastor may well begin with an inquiry into the experience each has had of the other's church. Have they experienced one another's churches? How does each respond to the theology, the liturgy, the sermons, the architecture, the totality of the experience in each tradition? How have they shared their responses? What role do the parents' wishes play in their decision? How has the couple approached the issue in their dialogue? If a decision has been reached about what church they will join, how has the decision been made and how satisfied are they with their decision? If the prospective bride and groom have failed to deal with this issue, it should be a warning sign to the pastor and the counselees that they are unable to share their feelings with one another and that there are unresolved issues at the very start of their marriage. The pastor is therefore challenged to direct the couple through this issue, to facilitate dialogue and understanding that they may affirm a common faith experience as a beginning of their Christian marriage.

In this regard there are survey instruments available which may be helpful to the couple, such as "A Religious Attitudes Survey" by William E. Crane and J. Henry Coffer, Jr. (Family Life Publications, 1964). Such aids can be very helpful as a starting point for those who are troubled by this issue. What must be avoided is the excess baggage of beginning a marriage with either partner feeling that he or she traded religious faith for love of the other or that he or she must save the other from an erroneous theological position and mode of expression.

Certainly, the ideal would be for the couple to receive instruction from clergy or lay counselors of both the churches involved regardless of whether or not clergy of both churches would participate in the wedding ceremony itself. While this may be the ideal, some churches would take definite positions which would preclude this approach; or, particularly in small towns, there may be personality problems among the local clergy.

The pastor should not assume that the couple must settle on one church. One couple comes to mind who attend both the Roman Catholic and Episcopal Churches, the traditions from which they had originally come, on the premise that when they married one another, each took on membership in one another's Christian families just as they became members of one another's natural families. They rejoice in their decision, which was reached with great care and love. This is not to say that there are no problems in such a resolution as a greater time commitment to the church is required of each, and there will be new problems arising if they begin to rear children in the church. How, for instance, will baptism, confirmation and the like be handled? This pattern is by nature schizophrenic and should only be entered into by mature persons with an extraordinary commitment to their faiths.

Perhaps no other issue so graphically illustrates the need for the pastor to schedule this series of conferences as far in advance of the wedding as possible as does the issue of mixed marriages. If the couple in a mixed marriage is going to deal adequately with the issue of their future commitment to the church, sufficient time must be allowed for both to experience in some depth the religious traditions of one another, to assess their own sys-

tems of belief and practice, to share their feelings with one another and finally, to come to an informed, loving, accepting and
creative decision.

Divorce

Because it is a question closely related to theological belief and
religious tradition, it is appropriate to close the discussion of the
question of the couple's relationship to their faith by raising the
question of how they feel about divorce. As the divorce rate approaches fifty percent, there is no escaping the issue. Each couple
coming to be married is probably aware of how easy it is to get a
civil divorce. Do-it-yourself divorce manuals and materials are
readily available in many communities. It is a probability that
the bride and groom have had some personal experience of the
problems of those who have been divorced through their family
or friends. The media tend to treat divorce very lightly, as a reality which comes into our lives as a matter of course.

Historically, the church has sought to follow Jesus' admoni-
tion not to divorce one's wife (Matthew 19: 2–9 and 5: 28–34)—
the question not having been put in terms of a wife divorcing her
husband—except in cases of adultery. Our Lord warned against
remarriage after divorce on the ground that if a man were to
marry another woman after making a vow to God on the occasion of his first marriage, he would then be guilty of breaking his
vow and, therefore, of adultery. Another assumption was that if
the man did not remarry he could then accept his former wife
back into his household should she repent of her evil ways. This
tradition was quite strictly adhered to in the ante-Nicene period
of the church's history. But by the time of Origen, the question
was being stretched to include divorce of women guilty of
witchcraft, infanticide and murder, circumstances which Origen
felt worthy of inquiry. As we have seen, from this early period to
the present, there have been very slow and subtle changes in the
practice of the church, if not in its specific teaching.

From the beginning, there were two issues involved: Divorce
and remarriage after divorce; and, just as today, intricate legal
arguments and local interpretations often differed from the
church's stated position. Always, there was the contrast between

the ideal laid down by Jesus and the particular situation of a person in extraordinary circumstances, a person for whom the church had a pastoral responsibility in the face of affliction. Historically, it must be remembered that the question of divorce and remarriage as we know it was often made moot by the untimely death of one party in a marriage. Life expectancy did not begin to change dramatically until the late nineteenth century with the discovery of the causes and cures of many fatal diseases. Until quite recently, very few couples grew old together. Today, life expectancy in the United States is 77 years for women and 69 years for men. In 1870 women could be expected to live only to the age of 38.5 years and men to 35.6. In Martin Luther's time, the average length of human life was only 25 years! Few couples were married long enough to face the many challenges to marriage found in modern society. Curiously, and perhaps tragically, it may be fair to say that the cost of divorce in human terms today is increasing in roughly the same proportion as the monetary cost of the health care which keeps us living longer and longer. While this matter will be discussed in greater depth later on, an astonishing phenomenon of our society is the incidence of divorce at the age of retirement, a pressure point of our human experience, circa age 65. The divorce rate of those 65 and older has doubled in the past ten years.[4]

Today, the church is in a great muddle over the issue of divorce and remarriage. While few churches would fail to accept a person who had been divorced, the American churches run the gamut from those which are strict and legalistic on both issues to those which, out of pastoral concern for the individual involved, take a more liberal and permissive position.

The canons on marriage after divorce in the Episcopal Church were changed radically in 1973. The intent was to remove the question from an essentially legal context to a more pastoral one. In the past such cases had been heard in a kind of ecclesiastical court in which the whole atmosphere sometimes verged on the Kafkaesque. The process now depends primarily upon the judgment of the local priest or deacon in whose pastoral care the person resides. The pastor is charged essentially with judging three matters: First, is the first marriage in fact dead and beyond hope of redemption; second, did the divorced counselee do all in his or her power to resolve the difficulties which led to the dissolution of the prior marriage; third, is the proposed marriage being entered into with a mature understanding of the meaning of Christian marriage? After due consideration and counseling on the part of the pastor, his recommendations are presented to the diocesan bishop and his council for final approval. In most cases, the judgment and recommendation of the local priest are accepted.

When divorce is viewed in pastoral terms, it is clear that it is very much a death-like phenomenon. If we understand death to be the end or radical change of a human relationship, divorce is death and the pastor must be prepared to help those involved with handling their grief. The work of Elizabeth Kübler-Ross[5] can be most helpful in post-marital counseling simply by substituting the word "divorce" wherever she uses the word "death." So often in divorce, all the stages of death identified by Kübler-Ross are present: denial, bargaining, anger, acceptance and withdrawal. The theological question becomes, if the church believes that it is appropriate for a person to remarry after the physical demise of a partner, why should it not be allowed in cases where the marital relationship itself has died? But, our Lord said that it is wrong. Interestingly enough, the United Methodist Church has proposed a service or liturgy in which the death of a marriage is recognized in the church—a kind of requiem for a marital relationship now recognized as being dead.

If a person cannot maintain the vows taken on his or her first wedding day before God and man, how can any future vow be taken seriously? How can a person value himself or herself as expressed in this most solemn utterance of his or her own marriage vow? This is a question to be discussed openly with the couple, recognizing that both human and marital relationships can die. As set forth in the third and ninth chapters of the Gospel according to St. Matthew, Jesus prohibits divorce, form criticism to the contrary notwithstanding. In order for the pastor to deal with the issue with the greatest candor, reflection upon his own anguish in coping with the tragic consequences of marital breakdowns may give helpful witness to the seriousness with which he takes his responsibilities in marriage preparation.

The Intellectual Facet

Still another facet of the marital love relationship to be examined in the individual interviews is how both parties feel about their intellectual compatibility. This is perhaps the least likely obstacle to a healthy marriage and is often among the easiest to indentify. We must be careful to distinguish between one's educational background on the one hand and one's ability to cope intellectually on the other. It is certainly true that the number of accumulated academic degrees is an inadequate measure either of a person's intellectual capacity or of his or her willingness to exercise the same. Similarly, there are many well-read and exciting intellects in our society whose formal education is quite limited. Because the use of the intellect is so important in communication as it relates to both expression and understanding, the intellectual compatibility of the two partners is crucial to the quality of their relationship. If this program is followed as it is set out thus far, the pastor should have a fairly clear idea of how able the bride and groom are to exercise their intellectual capacities with and for one another. In pursuit of greater clarity, the pastor may ask, "What kinds of things do you talk about? Do either of you read much; and, if so, what kinds of things do you read? Do you find that you share what you have read with one another?" As before, the point is for the pastor to impress upon the couple that this is an important facet of any human love relationship and that the couple must feel fulfilled and comfortable in this area as in all others. However, men and women who do not share a vocabulary or similar interests are not likely to be drawn together for they are less likely to meet; and, if they do, what have they to share during the developmental stage of their relationship?

Inter-cultural Marriages

Closely related to the question of the quality of the intellectual compatibility of two persons who would marry is the question of whether there is any great disparity in their cultural backgrounds. This is particularly an issue with marriages between persons from western and eastern or third world backgrounds. The issue is fairly clear but complex. If in marriage we are talking about taking on the whole person of another, there may be many cultural elements in the personality and *modus vivendi* of each party which the other simply cannot comprehend. How can we take on that which we cannot understand or fully appreciate? The fact is that as Christians we do it all the time, for none of us can fully comprehend the full dimensions of the Christ to whom we have pledged our love and our lives. The nature of the problem must be clarified and the problem itself must be faced.

Unfortunately, a problem which frequently accompanies such intercultural marriages is trouble with the parents of one or both partners. Objections from parents may have their origin in simple prejudice, feelings of cultural or racial superiority, fear of how the extended family and friends will respond or fear of a race or culture about which they know nothing or about which they have gross misconceptions. Certainly, there is the subconscious hope that one's grandchildren will be created in one's own image and the consequent fear of what one's heirs may look like. In any case, the dynamics of the feelings of the families must be faced squarely, for these too are part of what one takes on in the other. The pastor may find that conferences with the parents may be called for in such circumstances.

Seeking Help

The final step to be taken in the individual interviews is to offer some sort of guidance concerning when a person should seek advice and counsel on any personal or marital problems after the wedding. Here again the rate of failure of marriages in our culture should compel the pastor to encourage in every possible way either or both parties in a marriage to seek help when it seems appropriate. We must remember that while, on the one hand, psychiatrists, psychologists, clergy and counselors of every kind are reasonably well accepted as part of our health-care system, on the other hand, we are a country in which independence and individuality are highly-prized qualities. This is important to remember as such ideas of independence tend to militate against a person's seeking help when it is clearly needed. For many people, depending on counsel in the midst of difficulties is admitting to weakness within themselves. They may fear the stigma suggested by such old chestnuts as, "people will know you're crazy if you go to a shrink." The problem is that the image of sophistication to which many aspire may allow them to say they would seek help if they had difficulty, but they would in fact find it very difficult to pick up the telephone to make an appointment or walk in off the street to seek aid in coping with personal problems. The pastor's first responsibility is to help the person establish guidelines for seeking assistance.

As always, the questions used to lead off this discussion should be a series of inquiries providing a variety of approaches to the topic: "Do you know that the odds are close to even that your marriage will not succeed? And, recognizing the number of desperately unhappy people there are who remain married, unfortunately, chances are that the time will come when you will need help in your marriage, particularly at times of stress. How would you feel about going to get help if your marriage or an aspect of it was going badly? What kind of situation would prompt you to seek counsel? Where would you turn: To a clergyman, psychiatrist, psychologist, your mother?"

The key here might be to pick up any example the person might cite in response to this series of questions and to push him or her to extrapolate from that decision some more general guidelines which would be applicable to as many situations or combinations of circumstances as possible. It may be helpful to go back to his or her individual definition of love, to what the person stated he or she hopes to realize or celebrate in the upcoming marriage or to his or her reason for choosing to marry this particular person. These inimitable expressions may well provide a key to the beginnings of appropriate guidelines.

It is the experience of most pastors and counselors that people tend to seek help only after the dam has broken, when the accumulation of little or even big problems and annoyances have built up to the point where any viable life which may have survived in a marriage has been flooded by utter desperation. The pastor must point out the obvious: Seeking counsel to repair a damaged marital relationship makes so much more sense than attempting to rebuild completely that which has been destroyed.

The pastor must therefore encourage each person in the marriage to begin to formulate such guidelines, share his experience of the dreadful state of many of the persons who seek his counsel, remove any stigma which may be associated with the admission that help is needed and, finally, help the couple understand that there are many qualified persons, himself and others, who stand prepared to offer assistance to those in need. If we, the body of Christ, fail to communicate the extent of our concern for any person in need, our vocation is violated; and we should remove ourselves from the function of solemnizing the marriages of any children of God.

The session should end with an opportunity for the bride and groom to ask questions of their own and to reflect on what has taken place.

It is hoped that the reader will not be put off by the bulk of material which is recommended as necessary in these individual sessions. To be sure there are a number of substantial questions relating to the various elements of a loving and creative marital relationship which should be raised in a short time. However, while there are many questions to be asked, very few people are likely to have significant problems in all these areas. If there is a substantial number of such problems, the pastor may find it advisable, if not necessary, to encourage a reconsideration of either the wedding date or the marriage itself. But be not dismayed; most people are not all that traumatized, unsure of themselves or out of touch with reality!

:5:

The Final Interview

The final pre-marital conference with both the bride and groom should be timed very carefully. Sufficient time should elapse between the individual conferences and the final session to provide both bride and groom with an opportunity to reflect upon and share the experience of the individual interviews. If the pastor has done his job well, the counselees should have been provoked to considerable thought and conversation regarding themselves and their proposed marriage.

Following each of the previous interviews (not, of course, during the interviews) the pastor should have made notes on areas of concern, substantive discrepancies in points of view and the odd observation which he feels should be shared. It would be inappropriate to keep such notes on file after the wedding, although I must confess to wishing that I had kept some of the more interesting notes from my experience over the years for use in preparing this manual; but brief written notes are essential to the character and substance of this final conference.

Feedback

With his notes near at hand, but out of sight, the pastor may well begin the session with an open and non-directive question to test where the prospective bride and groom feel themselves to be regarding their relationship: "Well, tell me how you have spent the time since we last talked. Have you shared with one another your feelings after our talks? Have you discovered any differences which you would like to discuss, differences in your feelings or thoughts which you may not have been aware of before our conversations? What have you discussed about yourselves and one another? What are you excited about as a couple? What are the elements of your relationship or of the future which you would like now to celebrate?" Here the pastor might well take the opportunity to reassure the couple that it is quite impossible to settle everything before their marriage. Although a good healthy start is certainly well advised, marriage itself is a context for both raising and settling issues and problems, a time of considerate and sensitive confirmation of themselves and one another.

When these opening questions having been asked with assurance from the pastor that he does not expect any state of utopia to have been reached, it is time to listen with great care to what each has identified as a potential hazard or to what each has seen as confirmation of his or her decision. The pastor must also realize that there are matters which they may not yet have discussed in private with one another but have held back for discussion in the presence of the pastor, who may function as a buffer, a sounding-board or interlocutor. The counselor should be patient and willing to suffer a silence which may reflect reticence, reflection or hostility against self, the other partner, the pastor, parents or others. To respond effectively to what the couple may offer at this time will require every bit of the pastor's knowledge, skill, sensitivity, spiritual strength and experience. He must draw the two people out, observe their interaction with great care and be willing to offer his own reflections on any issue or question. Above all, honesty and carefully expressed candor are required. If issues or questions are raised by the couple which the pastor had previously observed and noted but had not yet himself articulated, a gentle confirmation that this matter had concerned him as well would be both helpful and well received.

The Pastor as Judge
There are two points in the premarital program at which, in my experience, one may be asked the question, "Do you think we shouldn't get married [at least not yet]?" This question is sometimes raised over the telephone but more often in person either following the individual interviews or near the beginning of the

final session. Because this question often surfaces at this stage in the process, a discussion of the decision-making role or power[1] of the pastor would seem appropriate at this time. Exercising my ministry as I do within the canons of the Episcopal Church and the provisions of civil law, my rule of thumb is that only for a grave cause should the pastor respond to that question with a "yes" or "no." The marriage of two people solely because the bride is pregnant may precipitate such a judgment of grave cause. The divorce rate in such marriages is much higher than in the population as a whole. Another situation would be a marriage between two people who are simply unable to make a valid decision because of the presence of some trauma in their lives. For instance, the recent death of the bride's father, a death as yet unaccepted, may drive the woman to seek another father figure in the man she is marrying rather than accepting him as a man who will be, in every sense, her husband. Gross immaturity or the inability of the couple to make a decision as reasonably stable, informed, rational and feeling persons may be still another circumstance constituting grave cause. Again, the divorce rate among those who marry as teenagers is far higher. However, in the absence of any grave cause, the decision must rest with the couple. The pastor must understand that if the prospective bride and groom should follow his affirmative advice and experience a fine and loving marital relationship until they are parted by death, they would be less able to celebrate their decision to marry as their own decision. Conversely, if the pastor's affirmative advice should be taken and the marriage turns out poorly or disastrously, the husband and wife could then blame the pastor and cop out on their own responsibility in the matter. If the pastor offers a negative opinion and the wedding is cancelled, the risk never being taken, the couple may hold the pastor responsible for breaking up a perfect union. To judge whether two people should marry is in a very real way to rob persons of their humanity. Remembering Harvey Cox's *On Not Leaving It to the Snake*,[2] the pastor can play the serpent role, tending to make decisions for others. He can participate in a process which causes people to fall short of the glory for which they were created. Each person's decision-making capacity is part of the glory of his or her creation.

It must be remembered that for clergy of the Episcopal Church, remarriage after divorce involves the exercise of an enormous amount of judgment as outlined in the marriage canons of 1973.

It is not an over-simplification to see the whole of this pre-marital counseling program as a process through which a couple passes in order to make its own decision. The ultimate decision may indeed turn out to be painful. If the program is taken seriously by all concerned, it is nonetheless as informed and considered a choice as possible, the kind of decision in which one may take pride and a measure of comfort and which may relieve one later of as many second thoughts as possible as to whether the decision was indeed valid.

The pastor, having listened to any thoughts or concerns which may have been identified by the couple, must then turn to his own notes without embarrassment or hesitation in order that any problem areas he may have identified may be discussed. Here again a light touch is in order, for the pastor is not prosecuting a case; he is reflecting on what he sees in a relationship which he will soon consecrate as a Christian marriage. He may begin by saying, "There are a couple of notes which I made following our individual conversations which bother me a bit, and I'm wondering if they point to topics that had occurred to you as possible issues which bear further consideration." Here the pastor must tread firmly but carefully. To quote one party against the other provokes anxiety and encourages defensiveness and hostility, and quite rightly so. However, simply to introduce the topic again so that each may share his or her response in the hearing of the other may well open an issue which has not been identified as a problem or potential problem because of the defense mechanisms of one or both of the parties or because of either party's lack of perception. The pastor must be careful not to raise any issues in such a way that he appears to be revealing the secrets of one of the parties. This is not easy, but it is vital.

Throughout the previous conferences, the couple will have been doing most of the talking. Not everything that needs saying can be covered through the reasonably non-directive approach outlined above. It may be helpful to the whole process to mention lightly but firmly at the onset that in the course of this, the final session, the pastor reserves the right as part of the contract to offer some of his own reflections on marriage in general. Again, he may remind the couple that everything he has to say should go without saying and that he certainly does not intend to insult the couple's intelligence or sensitivity. However, the accumulated experience of the church and society demand that it all be said even at the risk of insulting the intelligence of the counselees or offending their sensibilities.

What follows is essentially my own closing monologue very much as I share it with the couples whom I counsel. I have included some additional background material and reflections. It is considerably longer than usual: When writing, one tends to include everything. The point is, this is what I feel to be both important and effective. I share it in the hope that it will stimulate the reader to organize what he would share for the benefit of the couple and the marriage.

Reflections on Marriage

The pastor must begin with the clear and unequivocal statement of his belief in Christian marriage. If the pastor cannot speak with full assurance of faith and hope in this reality, then let him take his leave. For my part, to live outside of the community which my marriage offers to me—my wife, my children and our immediate families—would diminish the quality of my life immeasurably. My need would not be for a housekeeper, a lover, a nursemaid or a companion but for the community constituted in my marriage: Marriage as a context of love in confirmation and challenge, marriage as the locus in which to offer oneself as well as receive the offering of others, a union guided in all its activity, thought and feeling by the grace of God, with the power of the Holy Spirit.

Recognizing the ineffable character of the above, I am led to understand that marriage is by its very nature absurd.* I do not

---

* The use of the word "absurd" has been the subject of some considerable discussion with those for whom it conjures up images of Sartre and negativism in general. When one explains the proper use of the word as above, it is my experience that this line of discussion can be followed with very creative results. I reject the idea that one should allow writers and thinkers of former generations to prevent the use of a perfectly good word in our own generation.

use the word "absurd" lightly and certainly not in its popular sense of meaning "silly" or "useless." To me, the absurd is that which is beyond the capacity of reason, contrary to rational understanding or incapable of being sorted out by the intellect. Those who present themselves to be married are manifestly taking a risk. Fifty percent of the marriages any clergyman will consecrate may end in divorce, and it seems to me that to call marriage "absurd" is to define the character of the risk. It is only fair that the pastor share his perception of what it is the couple is taking on in their marriage; and while it may be unbridled love which is offered, risk is the context in which this love will be shared.

Individuality and Marriage

To the great misfortune of society, some churches have allowed to creep into the marriage rite a pseudo-liturgy in which three unlit candles are placed on the altar, one at each end and the third at the center. The "liturgy" which comes just before the blessing or benediction involves the bride and groom simultaneously lighting the two end candles which are then used by each partner to ignite the one candle in the center. So far so good, perhaps. Then a preposterous act is permitted in which the bride and groom extinguish the two candles which represent themselves: Demonic rubbish! To dramatize the extinguishing of the person clouds the reality of the whole idea of the marriage of two persons. When my wife and I married, I did not become "John-Ruth" nor did my wife then become "Ruth-John." We remain persons—individual creations of God who have chosen to be married to one another. Enter the absurd. Each party remains an individual, a person, yet no longer independent. Each person who has entered into the state of marriage becomes a partner in a new reality which, in a quite real sense, must be greater than the sum of the two parts. If this is not so, there is no need to marry. Cohabitation would be quite sufficient; and when and if one or both of the parties tires of the arrangement, someone moves out and another moves in. In marriage, a community of the faithful is somehow constituted by each pledging to the other all of whom and what one is. However, we must realize that to assert that the new reality is greater than the sum of the two parts is to speak in illogical, irrational terms, in absurd terms. In the face of all this we maintain our faith in the reality of marriage.

From This to Forever?

Suppose you were to ask any two people considering marriage, even those who have lived together for an extended period, to think carefully for a few moments and determine the amount of time, in minutes, which they have spent together, time spent truly together in spiritual, intellectual, emotional or physical union with one another and then place that figure, the number of minutes, over the total number of minutes of their life experience. Reducing the two figures to a percentage, they would soon realize that the resulting figure is shockingly small. On the basis of this tiny, tiny portion of their own total life experience and their experience of the other person, these two persons propose to stand up before one another, God, family and friends and pledge their total beings one to another until they are parted by death. I would submit that such a commitment is absurd: It is an undeniably irrational act, yet quite rightly taken with the utmost seriousness.

Change

Another example of the absurdity of marriage is found in a consideration of the phenomenon of change in our lives. Certainly, we all change in a variety of ways over the years. To encourage the prospective bride and groom to consider the extent to which they themselves have changed over the last five or ten years can bring the point home. How would each person's values, spirituality, goals, financial status, philosophy of life, emotional, intellectual and physical maturity, etc., compare with the other's over the years? Consideration of the changes in one's life over the past few years may give some indication of the extent to which change will occur within a marriage in the future. It is helpful to encourage both parties to consider what they know of how their parents have changed from the time of their marriage to the present. Consider how their parents will look in the couple's wedding pictures compared with the photographs taken on their own wedding days so many years ago. The changes in the thoughts and feelings of parents over ten, twenty or thirty years of marriage can be enormous and can introduce a note of helpful realism into the hearts and minds of any couple.

In addition to pointing out the manner in which looking at one's parents can dramatize how extensively a couple may change over the years, the pastor must encourage the couple to consider the fact that our parents are our primary role models not only in our lives as individual persons but also in our lives as marriage partners. When one considers the extent and character of change in every person over time, the absurdity of presuming to know the future reality of the person to whom one will be married in five, ten or twenty years' time becomes dramatically apparent.

Closely related to the issue of change is the factor of the frequency with which the average American family moves from community to community. While these figures include families in the military and those who may move from one apartment to another within the same building, statistics indicate that the average American family moves house every two and a half years! Growing together in a marriage in one place, on a farm, in a town or in one location in a city, is one matter. However, to have to adjust to such frequent changes in venue is yet another stress on all our relationships, not the least of which is the relationship one has to his or her spouse.

Sylvia Porter states that the average American male will have two and a half separate and distinct careers during his adult life, exclusive of education and military service. She quotes other authorities as saying, "In the closing years of the 20th Century, there will be an average of five to seven occupational changes in a typical lifetime."[3] A woman may think she is marrying a teacher, a plumber or a minister. In fact, she may be marrying all three. Although it is more difficult to sort out the jobs or vocations of many women (are homemaking and motherhood understood as jobs or vocations?), when one considers the radical changes in the roles of women in our society, it is quite clear that the statistics for women changing vocations might well be a great deal higher than they are for men. Taking all these factors into account, the assumption that one knows the person to whom one will be married in five, ten or twenty years' time is

presumptuous to the point of absurdity. The people sitting before the pastor must know and understand what all this may
mean in their lives.

Eden and Us

But let us go back to the beginning, as we must to comprehend
the archetypal marriage of the Judeo-Christian tradition, the relationship between Adam and Eve. The portrayal of the persons
in the garden, before the fall, is one in which all the characters,
God, Adam and Eve, are marked by two qualities: Total acceptance and total vulnerability. They all accepted themselves and
one another completely and without question. God was content
to be God and content to let Adam be Adam and Eve be Eve.
Eve was content to be Eve and content that God be God and
Adam be Adam. So also Adam was content to be Adam, content
that God be God and Eve be Eve. God walked about with his
creation in the garden in the cool of the evening while Adam
and Eve were "naked and unashamed." (Gen. 2: 25)

Their totally open acceptance of one another, naked and
unashamed, meant that they also lived out their lives in total
vulnerability to one another. In total acceptance, there can be
no posture of defensiveness: In practice, acceptance implies vulnerability. People created by the overflowing love of the Father
Creator, Adam and Eve were beings enabled by the power of the
same spirit which moved across the waters before the world was
made. Acceptance and vulnerability were the marks of their
creation. Maintaining this posture, they knew the nature of God
comfortably and naturally, complete in the glory with which
God had created them, created as they were in the glory of his
own image. And yet part of the nature of God, the glory of God,
was the capacity to make choices, to choose consciously between
one course and another, this being the same capacity of choice
out of which God had chosen to create them, man and woman,
at the beginning. This capacity of choice was what was ulti-
mately exercised first by Eve and then by Adam: Choosing between the state of grace—acceptance and the consequent vulnerability—and the act of partaking of the fruit of the tree of the
knowledge of good and evil, the fruit forbidden by God. But
what can be wrong with choosing to know the difference be-

tween good and evil even if it was the evil one who offered the temptation? Adam and Eve chose to turn from the glorious state into which God had placed them at creation to take second best, the law, which could never compare with their previous state. With the fall of mankind came also the fall of all institutions in which persons participate; marriage is among them.

What place can such a mythological statement as the fall of man have in our present understanding of marriage? The fact is that while there may have been arguments throughout the centuries as to the historicity of the account, while the exact nature of the myth, as myth, may have been argued, and while the interpretation of the account may have been subject to much discussion, the glory in which the relationship between Adam, Eve and God existed has always remained as the ideal for any man-woman relationship because they were blissfully with one another, naked and unashamed, at once accepting and vulnerable. The continuing task of men and women in relationship one to another is to strive to recover that same state of complete acceptance and vulnerability one with another. And here we find ourselves once again talking in absolute terms, the absolutes of acceptance and vulnerability negated by the fall, by the choice to live by law. As the result of the fall, we humans are incapable of reaching such absolutes by our own power; and yet to such an absolute we are called; to such absolutes we pledge ourselves in our vows at our marriage:

> In the name of God, I, *N.*, take you, *N.*, to be my wife [husband], to have and to hold from this day forward, for better for worse, for richer for poorer, in sickness and in health, to love and to cherish, until we are parted by death. This is my solemn vow.[4]

Such a pledge of exclusivity and permanence is all quite absurd but possible by the grace of God. It is no wonder that a pastor, in addition to being a celebrant in marriage as a clerk of the state, is a priest who calls upon God's grace:

> By the power of your Holy Spirit, pour out the abundance of your blessing upon this man and this woman.[5]

Without the participatory love of God, the fullness of the union cannot be known.

While the foregoing is my own perception of the reality of marriage, it is obviously not shared by all. It is imperative, however, that the pastor share his own interpretation of marriage with the couple. Where else can the couple be expected to turn for some personal, realistic, Christian teaching on marriage? While the pastor cannot be the answer person, he does have the responsibility to share the word of God, the *theo-logos* of Christian marriage with the couple.

A helpful analogy might be drawn from the pastor's own spiritual life, as each of us goes through periods when God seems far away, when our prayer life seems useless. These same types of low periods or desert experiences occur in marriage: Times when the relationship seems useless, unproductive or quite dead. Most clergy and lay counselors can relate to this phenomenon, perhaps in their marital relationship as well, and can witness to the death and resurrection experience in our relationships with God, neighbor and self: Experiences which, while tiresome, can precipitate exciting growth. We all know of couples who are all too anxious to respond to such times by giving up on the relationship in order to go it alone or seek a new start with a new partner. This is an experience to be faced head-on, anticipated from the start.

The Mating Dance

Moving on to other matters which should go without saying, it is important to point out that in their decision, the prospective bride and groom have withdrawn from the mating dance in which our society seems perpetually involved. While it is a rather extreme example, I recall the story told to my wife and me by our priest before our marriage. He recalled a couple he married one Saturday afternoon. All seemed to go well until about three weeks later when he received a telephone call from the bride, who was in a panic declaring that the marriage had been a terrible mistake and that she had to get out of it. Thinking that the groom must have been some sort of sadist or the like, he invited the bride to come right over to his study. It seems that the bride had resigned from her job just before her wedding and, upon returning from her honeymoon, had taken a position with another firm. There she had met a man whom she was convinced she could love far better than she could love her husband. Therefore she demanded an annulment or, if necessary, a divorce. The story illustrates the myth buried somewhere in our subconscious minds which declares that following our marriage vows there is some sort of automatic mechanism deep within our persons which relieves us of any attraction to members of the opposite sex, at least the kind of attraction which calls forth an active relationship. The woman may have been quite right in thinking that perhaps she could have loved the other man more than she could her husband. The fact of the matter is that she had taken herself out of the market, as it were. There will always be Robert Redfords, Farrah Fawcetts or folks down the block or at work to whom we could be attracted. Because of our choice to take our solemn vows we must not be attracted. While this example is rather humorous coming so soon after this particular woman's marriage, it is precisely the situation which is all too common later in marriage: The other woman or the other man.

Hidden Agendas?
Over the years, I have established the practice during the course of the final session of asking the couple to take one another by the hand and look into one another's eyes, as they will on their wedding day. It is interesting to note how difficult some couples find this. I say to them, "The person into whose eyes you are looking is the person you are marrying. If you have any ideas about changing the person into whose eyes you are now looking, whose hands you hold, if you have any hidden agenda as to how you plan to change this person, any agenda not as yet revealed to the other, let's call the whole thing off! To plan to change another person is in no way a part of marital love; it is manipulation which, by definition, is destructive. To harbor any such thoughts is dishonest; and dishonesty is no way to begin. Loose hands." That simple statement has called off more weddings in my experience than any other thought I have ever shared with a couple, any other question I have put to a couple, any issue I have raised, any homily I have offered or any survey instrument I have ever used.

Pressure Points

During the individual interviews, the pastor will have inquired of each party whether he or she has experienced any sexual relationships which might be termed traumatic, as such experiences have an extraordinary way of raising their ugly heads later in marriage. Similarly, there are many other less obvious traumas which may well affect the marriage over the years. It is quite impossible to catalogue all such potential hazards. However, the pastor should at least alert the couple to such phenomena and what they may mean in their lives. Rather than describing such events as traumas, it may be more helpful to describe them as "pressure points."

The first pressure point is the process through which the couple is now passing: The conferences on marriage and the wedding, the innumerable details involved with the wedding service and its accompanying festivities, the honeymoon or wedding trip, the establishment of a home and any changes in job or vocation which may call for yet more adjustments in the lives of the couple. There is not likely to be any other event in the lives of a married couple which so directly involves their parents as the planning of a wedding. This can be painful especially when the parents involved are particularly strong persons who are quite anxious to make their views known regarding the manner in which things are to be done. As previously noted, in situations where parents are divorced and remarried, the arrangements for the wedding can be particularly awkward. As will be suggested later, the pastor can be very helpful in making the wedding go smoothly, making it an event which can be celebrated and remembered fondly and clearly. Any assistance the pastor can offer the prospective bride and groom in their comprehension of the pressures under which they are living at this point in their lives is bound to be helpful. While the pastor cannot relieve the anxieties of the couple, perhaps he can help them understand what precisely it is they are going through by pointing out that the wedding and the bedding will soon be accomplished and the marriage may begin in wonder, joy and freedom in union.

From the time of the wedding onward, the pressure points at

which a marriage can be either enriched or broken become more evident in a quite insidious manner, each affecting some marriages more than others. In roughly chronological order, the obvious points are: The appearance of an ambiguously significant person from one partner's past; parental interference; moving house; financial straits; conception; pregnancy; the birth of children; completion of academic preparation; illness; death in one's family; changing jobs or vocations; the time when the youngest children enter primary school; entry or re-entry of the woman into the world of work (i.e., gainful employment); puberty of the children; the addition to the household of another person such as a parent, a cousin, a nephew; the time when the last child leaves the nest; and finally, retirement of one or both partners.

The Task-Oriented Relationship

Reviewing this representative list, one cannot escape comment on the manner in which marriage often becomes a task-oriented enterprise in which life is often wished away—"as soon as the children are in school, as soon as Grannie dies, as soon as Bob gets his raise or as soon as we retire: Then life will be better and we can finally settle down and enjoy ourselves." While we must recognize the ever-present vicissitudes of life, to understand the constituent elements of our married lives simply as tasks to be completed or problems to be solved in order that afterward married life can be enjoyed is to denigrate the potential joy of each stage or element of our married life experience. If life in marriage is reduced to completing this or that and if the two marriage partners fail to work together in the continual offering of the one to the other, when the tasks are completed, there may be no marriage left. A task-oriented marriage in no way prepares the parties for the future; it only destroys the present. Someone once said that the real trouble comes in marriage when the proper curtains are finally hung in the dining room.

Many of the pressure points may be most helpfully understood as death phenomena, again if death is understood as the end or radical change in a relationship. Moving from a community, changing jobs, sending children off to school at whatever stage, the wife's taking a job and retiring are primary examples.

Again we would commend the work of Elizabeth Kübler-Ross to the attention of the pastor and the couple.

One of the most common pressure points in our society, a time when marriage often fails, is when the last child has graduated from high school or college. It may more accurately be described as a time when there is a lack of pressure, for it would appear ostensibly that the reason for separations and divorces at this time is the absence of the necessity to provide a home for the children: a specific task. In fact, there is a more basic reason for marital breakdowns at this juncture. Such marriages tend to be those in which growth in the marital relationship has not taken place during the child-rearing years. The relationship between husband and wife in such instances is more habitual than conjugal, with the children being the *raison d'être* for the marriage. The family provides, if you will, the medium or bond between husband and wife which, when removed from the context of the home, raises the question, "why continue?" Marriage for the sake of the children is not marriage in any true sense. It is, however, an excuse for not coming to grips with oneself, one's husband or wife and the marriage itself. Understanding and coping with this all-too-frequent pattern is often obscured by a concurrent phenomenon, the return of the woman to the world of work. To be sure, such a decision on the part of the wife does require some considerable adjustment within any marriage. However, a marriage can adjust. A relationship which was once a marriage and has evolved into a cohabitation cannot.

One of the least understood pressure points is puberty. This time can be a very traumatic but unrecognized event in the lives of parents. Part of the reason is that we live in such a youth-oriented culture, in which the physical, youthful beauty of a person is so highly valued—hence, the extraordinary success of the cosmetic industry. A pubescent child in the household brings to mind how relatively old one has become. One sees one's children reaching that painfully glorious age at which they are suddenly attracted to members of the opposite sex. Natural feelings of physical attraction to our own children as attractive adults is automatically repressed by most people and the consequent frustrations are frequently manifested in the most destructive ways. The desire to recapture one's youth becomes paramount as one observes how old one's marriage partner has suddenly become. Precipitated by the maturity of their children, men and women often enter into secondary relationships in reaction to their personal confrontation with their own mortality.

Yet another pressure point is the time of menopause when the hormone balance of a woman can change so radically that she may become virtually a different person. In addition to the physiological problems, the psychological changes in her personality may present almost insurmountable problems to her marriage. Menopause is a particularly difficult problem in childless marriages as it marks the point beyond which bearing children is not simply improbable but impossible. Not as well understood is the phenomenon known as climacteric or "male menopause," which can be just as traumatic to the marital relationship.

Still another time of special vulnerability and danger, in some cases concurrent with menopause or climacteric, comes just before or at retirement. A great deal of mythology, often related to the task-oriented life style, has come to be associated with our expectation of what our retirement years will be like. Gerontologists generally agree that what a person has not experienced or practiced during one's working life, one will not be prepared for or able to do after retirement. Thus, many dreams for travel, rest, gardening, reading, etc., are dashed. Often, the vision of retirement each partner may have had is not shared by the other. The pressures of the child-rearing and working years may have protected the husband and wife from confronting their mortality and the reality of their stewardship of what they may have felt subconsciously was unlimited time. Such disillusionment can breed a terrible despair.

What can a pastor hope to offer the partners in premarital counseling with regard to the effect these pressure points may have on their relationship? He can only share his perception that the couple must be sensitized to what may lie ahead and to reiterate the absolute necessity for continued conscientious offering of oneself to the other while accepting the other and suffering the potential damage which might be wrought in such a vulnerable state. Certainly, a practical suggestion may be offered at this point in encouraging the couple to practice "preventive medicine" by anticipating these pressure points and, if there seems to be trouble ahead, getting to someone who can help.

Maturation in Marriage

One of the most difficult matters to deal with in the process of premarital instruction is encouraging the couple to make sure that they have some concept of maturing together in marriage. Here we are not talking about growing older together but growing together in marriage. I recall reading somewhere of a gardener in England who grew two trees, side by side. Each year he would take the new growth from each of the two trees and graft together two branches, one from each tree. Over the years he had grown a tree which he called a "ladder tree" for that was what it looked like, a live, growing ladder, strong and beautiful. The analogy may be weak, but there is some merit in it. So often a couple begins a marriage with what may be a strong, happy, fulfilling and enthused (in the theological sense) relationship: An organism, if you will, firmly planted and carefully cultivated. However, over the years as they suffer the vicissitudes of their individual and collective life experiences, they may fail to reach across to one another, to fuse their growth so that the organism can offer support to both of them and allow each to participate in the other's growth. So often we see couples who begin their adult life together and unconsciously grow apart, becoming increasingly separate organisms until one day they wonder whether or not they are indeed married. Too often we see such growing apart caused by the woman going her own way, starting or resuming a career or seeking to realize her own identity: What we might call the "women's liberation cop-out." The husband may hold to that dreadful idea that to keep a woman happy she should be kept in the bedroom or in the nursery where she belongs: "barefoot and pregnant." However, there are sufficient examples of fine, loving and creative marriages where the woman has grown considerably and in quite exciting ways in her professional life as well as in her life in her home with her husband and children, to the enrichment of both herself and her marriage.

Ministering as I do in an academic community with a very

large (5,000–7,000) married student population, I see quite the reverse situation occurring. The most frequent pattern is one in which the husband is taking courses, being stimulated intellectually and socially, accumulating academic degrees, moving in ever more exciting circles. During this period, his wife is left at home, quite often in a tiny, spartan and uncomfortable apartment. She is often the breadwinner in what may be a very dull and mundane job; and, perhaps, she is rearing children as well. In this case, the husband grows away, if you will, and the care for the ladder tree is left to another time: A time which often never comes. While the example cited is from an academic community, precisely the same phenomenon may be seen in the business community with workers, salesmen or executives who work to get ahead and succeed. The husband may progress while the wife is left behind. To avoid this pattern becoming destructive takes a great deal of dedicated work. What can the pastor offer? Only his reflections on his knowledge, experience and wisdom and a plea for awareness of this all too common pattern.

Decision and Closing

"Well, where are we? How do you feel about your proposed marriage after all this discussion?" The pastor offers the prospective bride and groom an opportunity to make their final decision about whether they should marry. To be sure, most couples are quite convinced of their decision before they ever call the pastor to arrange for their wedding, not yet comprehending that they will be called upon to pass through such a rigorous series of conversations about their marriage. By this point, however, if the pastor has made his offering conscientiously and if the two engaged people have lived up to the terms of the contract, they will have been through a great deal of soul-searching individually and together. They may have deep and well-founded reservations about their marriage. The pastor's responsibility and challenge is to allow them to decide in the negative without shame and with as little embarrassment as possible. Here the pastor must go back to the idea that while the two people may love one another quite profoundly, they must ask themselves the question whether or not their love for one another is a love which is of such a quality and quantity to warrant taking their vows, offering themselves in total acceptance and with total vulnerability one to the other, taking on one another "until they are parted by death." To call off a wedding takes guts. To be sure, there are instances when we recognize "unrequited love," when one party wants to marry and the other is reluctant to make such a commitment. However, a marriage cannot be built on the commitment of only one partner. With the exception of the foregoing circumstances, I have yet to experience a situation in which a wedding was cancelled or postponed and the couple did not soon feel pleased with their decision. Emily Post's book on etiquette provides not only all the necessary information on weddings, but also all the guidelines necessary for calling off a wedding at any stage. The primary message which the pastor must convey is simply that it is not only all right to cancel or postpone a marriage, but it may very well be a decision which, if carefully taken, is one to be commended and even celebrated. In such circumstances, the pastor should recognize his responsibility to follow up on both people involved and minister to them as needed.

The final interview ends with yet another opportunity for the prospective bride and groom to raise their own questions on any matters which have been discussed or any issues which may have been missed in the course of the interviews. If the budget has been discussed, there may be some questions regarding it or any other bit of specific homework assigned by the pastor, such as the Religious Attitudes Survey.

Once again, the pastor should not be discouraged by the bulk of material to be covered in this session. Just as no word in the English language can convey all its meanings at one time, the pastor will never find all these questions and issues relevant to every couple. However, it is important to recall that this session should be scheduled with no terminal point, no specific time when it should be concluded. And, finally, there may be rare cases in which yet another session will have to be scheduled, particularly when the two engaged people have serious doubts about whether they should be married.

:6:

The Rehearsal and the Wedding

We come at last to the rehearsal and wedding. Thus far, we have dealt exclusively with marriage. While any detailed discussion of the wedding should be postponed until as much of the marriage preparation is accomplished as possible, some matters regarding the wedding itself are bound to arise from the start. It is important to recall that the less said and done about the wedding, the easier it will be to postpone or cancel the marriage, should the bride or groom change his or her mind.

The date of the wedding is usually fixed in the minds of the bride and groom and their parents by the time of the first interview. During the first meeting between the couple and the pastor, the bare essentials of both the rehearsal and the wedding should be fixed: Date, time and place for both, numbers of attendants, approximate number of guests, decisions about organist and choir or soloist, flowers, venue of the reception, etc. The essentials should be set down as early as possible as well as handing out any policy and fee statement which the particular church may have established. Most important of all is for the pastor to put into the hands of the couple the different optional orders of services or liturgies which are sanctioned by the church and to raise but not settle the question of whether there will be simply the solemnization of holy matrimony or whether there will be a eucharistic liturgy as well. The reason for raising these liturgical options early and encouraging the couple to consider the options is twofold: First, to encourage the couple to begin to deal with theological and liturgical issues as early as possible; and second, to establish in their minds that the church and the pastor will be taking this part of the process as seriously as the consideration of marriage itself. There are bound to be anxieties about the service; and it is the pastor's responsibility to allay them and to make the wedding as joyous an occasion as possible, a day which the couple can remember fondly and clearly throughout the marriage.

Liturgy: Tradition and Invention

In any discussion of weddings, the first question is just how much latitude should the prospective bride and groom and their families have in altering extant services or in writing their own service? There is the clear danger that the solemnization of holy matrimony may become no more than a civil ceremony which happens to take place in a building owned by an organization called the church. I have been asked to officiate at weddings in the church using the 1928 Prayer Book Rite with all references to God, Jesus, Christ, the Holy Spirit and the Trinity removed. I have also been asked to follow the traditional rite but to omit either "until we are parted by death," considered by some to be too morbid, or the nuptial blessing. Needless to say I have refused to participate in such doings and have had couples turn to garden weddings with justices of the peace. If the couple, on learning what is involved in a church wedding, choose to go elsewhere and make other arrangements, fair enough. Everyone's integrity is better preserved; and while the bride or groom may disagree most strongly with the church's position, he or she may understand it better and respect it more. However, in such circumstances, there has always been for me a profound sadness. Our messianic consciousnesses aside, the church's responsibility is to be the church and the couple's responsibility is to respond in conscience.

One of the great advantages of *The Book of Common Prayer* is that in addition to the traditional Anglican rite, it provides "The Blessing of a Civil Marriage" and "An Order for Marriage" in which what the church considers to be essential in a wedding service is clearly spelt out. Any order which conforms to these criteria is permitted.

An Order for Marriage

If it is desired to celebrate a marriage otherwise than as provided on page 423 of this Book, this Order is used.

Normally, the celebrant is a priest or bishop. Where permitted by civil law, and when no priest or bishop is available, a deacon may function as celebrant, but does not pronounce a nuptial blessing.

The laws of the State and the canons of this Church having been complied with, the man and the woman, together with their witnesses, families, and friends assemble in the church or in some other convenient place.

1. The teaching of the Church concerning Holy Matrimony, as it is declared in the formularies and canons of this Church, is briefly stated.

2. The intention of the man and the woman to enter the state of matrimony, and their free consent, is publicly ascertained.

3. One or more Readings, one of which is always from Holy Scripture, may precede the exchange of vows. If there is to be a Communion, a Reading from the Gospel is always included.

4. The vows of the man and woman are exchanged, using the following form:

In the Name of God, I, *N.*, take you, *N.*, to be my wife [husband], to have and to hold from this day forward, for better for worse, for richer for poorer, in sickness and in health, to love and to cherish, until we are parted by death. This is my solemn vow.

or this

I, *N.*, take thee *N.*, to my wedded wife [husband], to have and to hold from this day forward, for better for worse, for richer for poorer, in sickness and in health, to love and to cherish, till death us do part, according to God's holy ordinance; and thereto I plight [give] thee my troth.

5. The Celebrant declares the union of the man and woman as husband and wife, in the Name of the Father, and of the Son, and of the Holy Spirit.

6. Prayers are offered by the husband and wife, for their life together, for the Christian community, and for the world.

7. A priest or bishop pronounces a solemn blessing upon the couple.

8. If there is no Communion, the service concludes with the Peace, the husband and wife first greeting each other. The Peace may be exchanged throughout the assembly.

9. If there is to be a Communion, the service continues with the Peace and the Offertory. The Holy Eucharist may be celebrated either according to Rite One or Rite Two in this Book, or according to the Order on page 401.[1]

For Episcopalians as well as others, these rubrics are clear concerning what is necessary for the celebration of a marriage in or by the church, offering considerable latitude while providing the pastor a clear reference as to what is required.

What is not outlined are the parameters of what used to be termed "seemly." That is, the pastor must still have clear in his mind what are appropriate readings, music and the like for use in the church on such an occasion. "Strawberry Fields Forever," with its implication of drug-induced happiness, or "Roll Me Over in the Clover," with its crass emphasis on recreational sexuality, would be constituted inappropriate as would some writings by Sartre or Ginsberg. The trouble comes in the vast mid-range of material which some couples seem to care for, such as readings from the Rhubaiyat of Omar Khayyam or the singing of the "Wedding Song." All the pastor can do is to test whether such extra-biblical or untraditional bits and pieces in the context of the whole liturgy overpower or substantially detract from the essential Christian message concerning marriage. In the final analysis, a good case can be made for the direct participation of the prospective bride and groom in designing their own service, within the above guidelines. The words we ourselves write are closer to us than those which we hear or read. An intimacy may be realized which may be truly a wonder. Yet the process is fraught with dangers, the most common ones being rank sentimentality and unbridled secularization.

The Shape of the Liturgy

Having put the various optional services into the hands of the couple for their consideration and having spent a number of hours with the couple, the pastor then reviews the service with them. The essential teaching about the service is at the heart of what we do as pastors, and so it comes in the order in which it does. Just as there is a specific shape to the eucharistic liturgy, so also there is traditionally a theological and rational shape to the form of the service of holy matrimony. It is not unlike what we were taught in school about public speaking: You tell them what you're going to tell them; you tell them; then you tell them what you have told them. In discussing the wedding service, first we talk about what we are going to do and why we are going to do it; then we do it; then we reiterate what we have done by praying that the marriage entered into by these two persons, supported by all present, including God, will succeed in every possible way.

Following the traditional entrance of the guests and wedding party into the church, the service opens with a theological and historical rationale for marriage. The primary message is that the church takes marriage seriously. The marriage takes place in the sight of God and in the company of the faithful. God is involved. According to the fourth gospel, Jesus celebrated his first miracle at a wedding. St. Paul, apostle, teacher and pastor, reiterated the seriousness of marriage and likened the marital relationship to that which exists between Christ and the church. The purposes of marriage are then enumerated: Mutual joy, help and comfort in good times and bad and, if it is God's will, the procreation of children and their growth in the Lord. As it says in *The Book of Common Prayer*, "Therefore marriage is not to be entered into unadvisedly or lightly, but reverently, deliberately and in accordance with the purposes for which it was instituted by God."[2]

An opportunity for anyone present to raise objections is provided and one final charge to the couple is made, offering them one last opportunity to change their minds.[3] It is at this point in the proceedings that there is a traditional confusion or a confused tradition. I would wager that if you were to ask married members of your congregation to repeat their wedding vows, they would confuse the betrothal, or statement of intention, with the wedding vow:

> *N.*, will you have this man [woman] to be your husband [wife]; to live together in the covenant of marriage? Will you love him [her], comfort him [her] , honor and keep him [her], in sickness and in health; and, forsaking all others, be faithful to him [her] as long as you both shall live?[4]
>
> *—betrothal or statement of intention*
>
> In the Name of God, I, *N.*, take you, *N.*, to be my wife [husband], to have and to hold from this day forward, for better for worse, for richer for poorer, in sickness and in health, to love and to cherish, until we are parted by death. This is my solemn vow.[5]
>
> *—wedding vow*

This confusion is partly due to the lack of effective teaching on the part of the church over the years as well as to the manner in which Hollywood has presented weddings on the screen. The former, the betrothal, is simply a statement of intention, read by the celebrant, to which the bride and groom in turn give assent, "I will," which is in the future tense. Over the centuries, this statement of intention was sometimes made years before a wedding and even, in some cases, by parents before the bride or groom was conceived. In our present day, it is something of an anachronism and is titled "The Declaration of Consent" in *The Book of Common Prayer* but is still included as a condition for marriage in the rubrics given above. As with so many rites of the Christian tradition, it has been reinterpreted and now is considered to be the proclamation of the bride's and groom's realization that they know what they are taking on in marriage and are doing so of their own free will.

The theological rationale having been given, the last opportunity for objections or withdrawal having been offered, the couple having stated their free intention to marry, the members of the congregation, all those who have been invited to witness the wedding and support the marriage, are called upon to proclaim their support:

> *Celebrant:* Will all of you witnessing these promises do all in
> your power to uphold these persons in their marriage?
> *Response:* We will.[6]

This is a very important action; for as we have seen, the couple will need all the help and support they can possibly receive throughout their marriage. The congregation is not simply a group of guests but is in fact a body of witnesses and supporters of this marriage, in a sense assuming the role of "godparents" to the couple. This liturgy is the action of the whole church.

In the revised liturgy of the Episcopal Church, a familiar question, "Who giveth this woman to be married to this man?" has not just been made optional but has been made a secondary footnote; and provision has been made for what amounts to a three-quarter turnabout in the practice with the words, "Who presents this man and this woman to be married to each other?" In the past, the father of the bride or some appropriate male substitute gave the bride to the church, which then gave her hand to the groom. Clearly this tradition derives from a time when a daughter was essentially chattel, that is, the property of the father who gave her, at worst, as he would a horse in trade, or, at best, as his beloved daughter, blood of his blood, flesh of his flesh, to one who promised to love and cherish this woman for the duration of her life. This matter grates on many brides and grooms in our time and for a good reason. The bride, after all, is not chattel or a piece of property, but a person, yet one who is coming from others—her parents, people whom she loves. But she is now to be married to another, leaving one community for another as is most appropriate. Is it possible to reinterpret the symbol of the "giving away of the bride" in a creative way? I think so, but only for some. A symbol only becomes what one makes of it. While its origins may be perverse, its modern use may indeed be loving.

It is appropriate that the congregation be instructed by the word of God read from scripture. While a homily or sermon is not required, it is most certainly appropriate and, indeed, an obligation for the pastor. The congregation must be made aware of its responsibility to witness this marriage and support it in the years to come, "for better for worse, for richer for poorer, in sickness and in health . . . until [they] are parted by death." In the homily or sermon, the pastor must be clear and concise and speak of the good news which our Lord brings to this relationship. To fail to preach the gospel to those who have gathered for such an occasion would be for me unconscionable.

Having said all there is to say, the marriage itself takes place: "in the name of God, I, John, take you, Ruth, to be my wife. . . ." The rings are blessed and exchanged.[7]

Finally, all who have gathered pray for the marriage, the families, the children (if appropriate), the church and the world. The wedding concludes with the nuptial blessing.

The Eucharist

Here it is appropriate to consider whether there should be a eucharist. If we are gathering to witness the vows, to pray for the marriage and to bless it, it would seem to me most appropriate to celebrate the greatest prayer the church has to offer, that is, the eucharistic prayer. Offered in response to our Lord's imperative, "Do this for my remembrance," the great thanksgiving or eucharist is appropriate because it is the central act of Christian worship and because the church should offer whatever it possibly can in support of every marriage. Certainly the idea of thanksgiving is most fitting in this setting in which we offer gratitude for both the love of God, which is dramatized in the eucharist, and for the loving union of two children of God. Resistance to the idea of a "nuptial mass," to use the traditional phrase, is rather curious. It seems to relate to the old prejudices about popery and the like. Many couples prefer a quickie: going into church, saying the "I do's" and leaving. The problem once again seems to be related to the question of educating our people about the historic tradition of the church and the nature of the eucharist itself. What could be more fitting than for the bride and groom's first action after their marriage to be the offering of themselves to God at the altar and the receiving of the body and blood of the one who came to redeem all relationships? The couple should at the very least have the option carefully explained to them.

Because of their sensitivity to their wedding guests, who may include atheists, agnostics, and Jews, as well as Christians who may be made to feel out of place in such a liturgical setting, many brides and grooms may wish to celebrate the eucharist and protect their guests from feeling awkward. In such instances, it would be quite appropriate to suggest a pre-nuptial eucharist, that is, a small gathering of family and friends for a simple liturgy on the morning of the wedding. However, the personal integrity of the couple is more important than the comfort of the guests.

After a review of the service, an explanation of its shape and meaning and an encouragement to the couple to celebrate the eucharist, the most comforting words the couple can hear from the pastor are, "Trust me. We will rehearse the ceremony carefully and I will tell you exactly what to do at every stage during the service." After all, the only words the couple must commit to memory are, "I will" (not, "I do," as in the Hollywood version) in response to the declaration of intention. For the remainder of the service, they only repeat after the celebrant or read from the prayer book or printed service. A question which often comes up is whether the prospective bride and groom care to memorize their vows. Many couples feel it is too awkward to repeat them after the celebrant. The experience of many clergy is that if the bride and groom attempt to offer their vows from memory, they think of little else, wondering if they will remember them. Weddings provoke sufficient anxiety without having this added on. Should the bride and groom insist on taking their vows from memory, the celebrant may alleviate considerable distress by having the vows typed out on a card which can be inconspicuously offered should either the bride or groom falter.

The Rehearsal

While it is certainly true that each clergyperson has his own way of conducting a wedding rehearsal, my knowledge from a variety of sources is that few clergy make a rehearsal all that it may indeed be and that still others convey a feeling of contempt for having to spend time in this way. What is forgotten is that a wedding rehearsal is an opportunity for ministry. This ministry is primarily to the bride and groom and only secondary to all others who are involved. Too frequently the rehearsal is simply a clerical recitation of "this is what you do, what you say and where you stand."

How can ministry happen in such a context? The first matter to be communicated with regard to the wedding, as well as with regard to the whole of the premarital conference process, is that the church, through the pastor and whoever else may be involved, takes the matter of the wedding very seriously. If the pastor has spent a number of hours with a couple seeking to prepare them for as happy and creative a marriage as possible, so also should he offer the same ministry of preparation regarding the wedding. Thanks be to God that it doesn't take as many hours! I am convinced that much of the popularity of the tradition of spending vast sums of money on wedding photographs is simply due to the fact that the bride, groom, family and attendants are so traumatized by the wedding that they have to buy the photos to make sure in their own minds that the wedding did, indeed, take place. The celebrant must communicate to the couple that the purpose of the rehearsal is to make sure that all concerned know *what* they are to do and *why*. The purpose of a wedding rehearsal is not to put on a show but to prepare in order that the wedding may be a fine, relaxed celebration of the beginning of marriage.

Another way in which ministry can occur in the rehearsal is to integrate the rehearsal of liturgy as much as possible with the content of the discussions of marriage. For instance, if we say we believe that the bride and groom are the ministers of the sacrament, make certain that they speak their vows to one another, hand-in-hand, face-to-face, and not to the celebrant. Make sure that they speak up! The congregation has gathered to witness the vows and to pledge its support of the marriage in the years ahead. It is only appropriate that the congregation be permitted to hear the vows it is to witness. If we agree that the liturgy is not simply a show, encourage the congregation to participate in the prayers. The liturgy is a dramatic presentation; be clear in your own mind of what is dramatized.

The preliminary preparations for the rehearsal begin at the first meeting with the two engaged people by the pastor suggesting in the strongest possible terms that they arrange to have the whole wedding party present for the rehearsal. Missing attendants who breeze in at the last minute are cause for precisely the kind of anxiety which militates against a good memory of one's wedding, not the least part of which is the vows about which so much has been said. A vow taken is nothing if it is not a vow recalled.

The rehearsal should take place as close as possible to the wedding date so that those involved may remember the part each has to take in the ceremony.

The hour should be chosen with two things in mind: First, that it be a time when the whole party may in fact assemble on time; second, that it not be preceded by any festivities the nature of which may dull one's senses; I speak of cocktail parties, bachelor parties and the like. The rehearsal is crucial, and the pastor is the one person who knows sufficient horror stories to impress the couple with its importance.

As has been stated, the rehearsal is a time for ministry. After all have assembled, the occasion should begin with a prayer, after which the pastor talks through the service explaining its essential theological character, the shape of the liturgy and why, briefly and clearly, we do things as we do.

However, before there is any rehearsal, as such, there is one crucial role the celebrant has which in most cases only he can perform. He must impress upon the whole wedding party that they have been honored to have been asked to participate (remember, the maid or matron "of honor") and further that they are attendants and it is their duty to *attend*. The members of the wedding party are there to assist the bride, the groom and their families in whatever way possible, to be on the spot and to fulfill their responsibilities, whatever is asked of them. Too often the emphasis of those in a wedding party is on the word "party," an understanding which has led to some embarrassing moments, great anxiety and unpleasant memories of what should be a solemn but joyful experience for all. The bride and groom cannot play the "heavies" and stand before their families and friends and shout, "attend!" The celebrant can and must. And how such a direct appeal to all is appreciated by the bride and groom, not to mention the ubiquitous mother of the bride! Similarly, the pastor may give specific directions concerning the time each member of the party should arrive at the church in a far more forceful manner than may the bride or groom. We all know that wedding guests like to arrive early to get the best seats and what an embarrassment it is when the guests arrive before the ushers.

On Photographers

Wedding photographers are quite capable of being like bad funeral directors who would assume absolute control of the service if given an opportunity. In their minds, the wedding is staged for their personal artistic expression or even exploitation; and they could not care less about the theological content of the rite, the meaning of the vows or the comfort of the wedding party, the family or the guests. I shall never forget a marriage solemnized by me in which an obviously well-prepared family, during the reading of the introduction, produced from beneath their clothing bits and pieces of a movie camera: One family member had the camera itself; one, the battery pack; and two others, parts of a light bar which they adroitly assembled. Suddenly, during the charge to the bride and groom, the lights came on not eight feet from the chancel steps, and the camera began to grind away. I was totally blinded and had to stop the ceremony, step down to the front pew and tell the family that the ceremony would not continue until the entire apparatus had been put away. After the service, the family's comment was, "Well, you only said, 'no flash bulbs.' "

Two rules must be set down: First, no flash or floodlights, noise or intrusion during the service, defined as from the beginning of the entrance hymn or prelude to the departure from the nave of the mother of the groom; second, a strict time limit on the taking of photos following the service. I have experienced one wedding where the great high priest of photo magic kept 250 guests waiting one hour and forty-five minutes at the reception while he ran roughshod over all concerned, causing great anxiety and anger in everyone. These rules should be communicated to the couple for careful transmission to the photographer during the planning stage of the wedding, and the celebrant should reiterate the rules to the photographer personally just prior to the wedding.

From the beginning of the discussion of the wedding, through the rehearsal and during the ceremony itself, the pastor offers all in his power to relieve anxiety in everyone in order that the occasion and the vows of all concerned may be recalled clearly and happily.

Afterword

It is unfortunate but true that the pastor must face squarely the prospect of failure. The old saw "marriages are made in heaven" is frequently used as an excuse for not accepting our responsibility as pastors in this ministry of premarital counseling. However, there is a grain of truth in this statement in the sense that the best-prepared, the most devoted, the most diligent pastor may fail in his attempt to prepare a couple for a fulfilling marriage. In any marriage there are three major components: The bride, the groom and the world, including all who dwell therein. Weakness, disease or lack of understanding or commitment in any of the three may cause the marriage to fail. The pastor is not the messiah but only a messenger of the good news of redemption.

I recall three quite significant failures in my own experience. The first involved a very young couple from near the Scottish border whose accent was so thick, whose educational background was so limited and whose ability to cope with my American accent so understandably limited that communication could barely take place. We laughed about our problem and did the best we could. I investigated the possibility of referring the couple to another priest but, for a variety of reasons, this was impossible. I have never heard from this couple and do not know how they have managed. I felt quite a sense of failure in that instance in which circumstances beyond our control had defeated our efforts to such a large extent. The second example involved two young people who were simply dishonest with me, with one another and with themselves. In this case, the bride was pregnant and would not share this fact with me. Furthermore, the marriage was being forced by the parents of the groom; and the couple simply lied about their financial status. I did my best, but the marriage ended disastrously. The third couple was entirely ill-equipped to deal with ideas, challenges or the experience of others. As pastors, we must face the fact that the program outlined in this work will be for many men and women the most trying intra- and inter-personal exercise they have ever undertaken, an experience for which they may be totally unprepared. I recall raising the issue of sensitivity with the bride of this third couple. Her response was that, while both were well educated, she and her fiancé neither understood nor valued sensitivity for each other. That couple is now in the process of a divorce. The pastor cannot hope to provoke human development where there has been none in the past. The pastor makes his offering in the hope that, by the grace of God, an exclusive, permanent love relationship will result.

The reader will note that this program does not deal with questions of parenting. Given the pressures under which we all live, there are limits to what we may hope to accomplish with any couple. As has been mentioned, the bride and groom should be encouraged to seek counsel when it is required, both regarding unanticipated problems and pressures in their relationship and regarding the rearing of their children. Increasingly, programs on marriage enrichment and parenting are offered by the church and secular agencies. Such programs should certainly be commended to every couple. The pastor should always assume a continuing responsibility for the pastoral care of those whose marriages he has solemnized. Calling on each couple two or three months after the wedding is much appreciated and can be very helpful. However, in our transient society, this may prove impossible. In most cases, a brief letter of commendation to a colleague in the new community of the couple is possible. It is certainly appropriate!

A Proposal
I am sure that I am not alone in my disillusionment over the financial compensation received for premarital counseling.

Please do not misunderstand: I believe in this ministry and I enjoy it! However, I am distressed to know that as the result of many hours of hard work and years of preparation, clergy generally receive less for weddings than do organists, soloists and sextons, not to mention caterers, dressmakers, florists and tuxedo rental agencies. I am well aware that as a priest of the church, I should not profit personally from "stole" fees. However, the church, through all its members, supports me in my ministry. The church supports me in order that I may minister; premarital counseling is part of my ministry.

My proposal is simply this: There should be no charge made by the parish or the clergy to any persons being married who personally support the church as they are able or whose families support the church as they are able. However, if the church, through clergy and lay counselors, conscientiously provides premarital counseling to those who do not support the church with their attendance and their monetary gifts, the church should then ask the bride, groom and their families seriously to consider tithing to the church ten percent of all expenses relating to the wedding. Such gifts would then help to underwrite the continuation of the vital ministry of premarital, marital and post-marital counseling. Is this not reasonable?

This proposal could be written as a policy statement including a work sheet listing all costs on the basis of which the tithe would be calculated. It could then be given to every couple along with any other relevant rules and regulations with no more being said. Any family which spends $1,000.00 on a wedding should certainly be prepared to contribute $100.00 to the church so that its ministry in this vital area may continue. In like manner, a couple with but $50.00 to spend should only be asked to contribute $5.00.

The added benefit for the couple and the family is that they may be better aware of just how much money they are committing to the festivities which accompany this marriage.

Appendix A
Summary of Content of Program

I. The Initial Interview
  A. Establishing credibility:
    1. Pastor takes all this most seriously.
    2. Personal belief of pastor in sanctity of marriage.
    3. Pastor's commitment of time, energy, experience.
  B. Explanation of process:
    1. Four sessions—First with couple, second and third with individuals, fourth with couple.
    2. Discussion will be about the various facets of a marital-love relationship.
    3. Purpose: To encourage them to articulate their understandings to themselves and one another—not to the pastor.
    4. Format: Mostly raising questions and issues for their discussion and, at the end, the pastor's sharing of his own experience.
    5. Caveats:
      (a) Every question asked and every issue raised should go without asking or raising. Experience dictates that it will be covered and that the couple understands it is not being singled out.
      (b) The discussion will be on marriage; only at the end will the wedding be discussed.

C. The contract:
1. Time—at least four hours with the final session open-ended.
2. Energy—this is hard work and challenging.
3. Honesty—without which the effort would be useless.
D. Does the couple agree to the contract? If response is affirmative:
1. Complete information forms.
2. Schedule interviews (last one open-ended).
3. Hand out policy and fee schedules.
4. Set rehearsal time and place—insist on all parties present and on time.
E. Questions and comments:
[After Initial Interview, pastor makes notes on any issues, reactions or feelings to be picked up in later sessions.]

II. The First Interview (*Both bride and groom present*)

A. Reiterate terms of the contract and test enthusiasm.
B. Begin to establish the fact that you are a good listener.
C. Getting to know one another:
1. "Tell me about yourselves: Where do you come from; where are you headed; how did you meet and when?"
2. The pastor introduces himself, briefly establishing his experience and credentials.
D. Questions and issues for discussion:
1. "Why do you want to be married in the church?"
2. "Why marry at this time?" (Pregnancy?)
3. "Why marry this person?"
4. Pick up on language of responses:
(a) "What about love?"
    i) How each uses the word or fails to use the word.
    ii) Character and quality of the love expressed.
    iii) Define "love."
(b) Deal similarly with other words or phrases used in response to opening questions.
5. "Have you had intercourse *with one another?* We want to get this out in the open."
6. "If so, are you living together on a full- or part-time basis?" If "yes,"

(a) "What does living together mean to you?"
(b) "Why get married?"
(c) "How does marriage differ from living together?"
7. "What are your ideals of marriage, your mental image of the married state?"
8. "Whose marriages form the model for your own?"
9. "Describe your relationship to your parents and future in-laws. How do they feel about your marriage?"
10. "Describe your parents' marriages."
11. "How do you see your parents' marriages affecting your concept of marriage?" (role models)
E. The couple's questions and comments.
F. "How are we doing with the contract?"
G. Give couple copies of authorized liturgies for its consideration.

[After the First Interview, the pastor makes notes on any issues, doubts, questions, reactions or feelings to be picked up in later sessions.]

III. The Individual Interviews

Caveat: Second (or third) marriage; age differences (see III, C, 10).
A. "Any questions or comments before we begin?"
B. "What have the two of you discussed since our meeting? If nothing, why? What was the tone of the discussion?"
C. Facets of a marital love relationship:
1. Introduction:
(a) How do the two people spend their time together and apart?
(b) How do they decide?
(c) What does each do that the other does not enjoy?
(d) How are separate interests perceived by each?
2. Communication:
(a) General communication—
i) How do the two people perceive the manner in which they communicate?
ii) How well do they and the pastor feel they know one another?
iii) How have they learned about one another?
(b) Conflict—
i) What do they fight about?

    ii) How is conflict resolved? (review last fight or disagreement)

    iii) If no fights, why?

3. Psychological facet:
   (a) How would each characterize themselves and one another in psychological terms?
   - i) Dominant/Submissive
   - ii) Aggressive/Passive
   - iii) Rational/Intuitive/Feeling
   - iv) Strength of *anima/animus*
   - v) In any other terms

   (b) How consistent are these patterns?
   - i) How do they feel about the combination?
   - ii) What role do their psychological types have in their choice of one another?
   - iii) Extract an example, e.g., relationship with parents, for discussion of how their "types" are lived out when together and apart.

4. Role definitions:
   (a) How does each view their role in the marriage?
   (b) What effect has the women's movement had on their vision of their marriage?
   (c) Do they disagree about their roles?
   Suggest writing out a "duty roster" starting with what each wants to do.

5. Physical/sexual relationship:
   (a) What is their physical relationship like with one another?
   (b) What is their sexual experience with others?
   (c) How do they see the role of sex in their relationship? (recall types of sexual activity)
   (d) Review relationship of sexuality to intimacy—knowing and knowing about the other.
   (e) Are there distasteful aspects?
   (f) Are there guilt feelings?
   (g) Is the sexually active woman orgasmic?
   (h) How well do they communicate to one another their sexual desires and feelings about sexual activity (sensitivity)?

(i) Has each discussed with the other his or her past sexual experience, and how comfortable is each with his or her decision?
    i) Is there sexual trauma in their backgrounds? Consequent feelings?
    ii) Is a referral called for?
(j) What about masturbation?
    i) How do you feel about it? (guilt)
    ii) What role will it have after marriage?
    iii) Sexual fantasies
(k) Hang-ups
(l) What do they know about family planning?
    i) How have they learned?
    ii) What decisions have been made?
(m) Both should have complete physicals.

6. Finance:
  (a) Present and projected financial picture?
  (b) Discuss—
    i) Budgeting
    ii) Expenditure limits
    iii) Sources of income
    iv) Life insurance
    v) Balance in, as well as of, the family budget
  (c) How was budget determined and by whom designed?
  (d) Who will keep the household accounts and pay the bills?
  (e) Offer budget forms for their use.
  (f) Suggest financial planning resources in the community.

7. Spirituality:
  (a) Relationship to God, Christ and church
    i) Why has the couple come to the church to be married?
    ii) Where are they in their relationship to God, Christ and church?
    iii) Help to define religion and faith in the body of christian fellowship.
    iv) What are their levels of spiritual sophistication?

     v) How has each shared his or her feelings and experience in this area?

     vi) What is the church background of each?

     vii) Encourage a mature decision and commitment in this area.

(b) Mixed marriages:

     i) Not to be an excuse for avoiding this issue!

     i) What is their experience of one another's church?

     iii) What has been decided and how? (possible use of Religious Attitudes Survey).

     iv) Review possible patterns of church involvement in mixed marriages.

(c) Divorce:

     i) Church's ideal and pastoral concern.

     ii) What has been their experience of divorce in family and friends?

     iii) This question is not to be taken lightly— see divorce rate and pressures of our age.

8. Intellectual facet:

(a) Review educational background and expectations of each party.

(b) If disparity exists, how do they feel about it and deal with it?

     i) Review relationship of intellect to facility in communication.

     ii) What do they read, discuss, share in the world of ideas?

(c) What degree of comfort do they feel in this area?

9. Cultural facet:

(a) Is this a marriage of persons from different cultural or racial backgrounds?

(b) How much does each understand about the other?

(c) Reaction of parents to inter-cultural or -racial marriages to be reviewed.

(d) How well does each understand the feelings of the parents?

(e) Would conferences with the parents be helpful?

10. Age differences:
    (a) If ages of parties are quite different, how well does each party understand the implications?
    (b) How have they discussed this with one another?
    (c) What does the future look like?
        i) Sexual relationship.
        ii) Likelihood of long widowhood.
        iii) Review the question of remarriage after death of spouse without guilt.
        iv) Reaction of families to such a marriage
D. When to get help (counsel) for your marriage:
    1. The risk is great and chances are every couple will need help at some point.
    (a) What are the guidelines?
        i) Only in crisis.
        ii) At times of pressure.
        iii) As "preventive medicine."
    (b) Discuss need to overcome reticence to seek aid.
    (c) From whom would the couple seek help? Review resources.
E. Questions or comments from bride or groom
    [After each individual interview, the pastor makes notes on any issues, doubts, questions, reactions or feelings to be picked up in final session.]

IV. The Final Interview
A. Prior to meeting with couple, review all notes from previous meetings.
B. Reflections and questions from the couple: Inquire into what the couple has shared or discussed since the individual interviews.
    Introductory questions:
    1. "Do you see any problems or facets of your relationship you had not noted before?"
    2. "What have you realized that you have to celebrate since our conversations?"
    3. "Are there any issues or questions which I might help you discuss together today?"

C. Items for the pastor to note:
1. How has the attitude of the couple changed over the interim?
2. What is their mood toward one another and toward the pastor?
3. Why?
D. The pastor brings out his notes on areas which he believes require further exploration.
1. He then raises these with the couple—not quoting one person against the other.
2. Be prepared to be quiet and let them think.
[What follows, through E, 10, is the author's outline of what he would share. The reader is encouraged to outline his own presentation.]
E. The pastor's thoughts and experience on marriage:
1. Witness once again to your own belief in marriage.
2. Raise the issue of the absurdity of marriage, as "absurdity" defines the risk involved.
Examples of absurdity:
(a) Divorce rate/"till we are parted by death."
(b) Individuality in marriage (the candle "liturgy").
(c) Marriage as greater than the sum of the parts.
(d) Time spent together as compared to total lifetime.
(e) The reality of change of persons in marriage:
i) How has each changed in the last five years?
ii) Look at change in their parents' marriages.
iii) Role definition change over the years.
iv) Examine the effect of our transient society and multiple vocations or careers.
3. Discuss the ideal of Adam and Eve—"naked and unashamed"—open, accepting, loving, vulnerable.
4. Discuss the mystery of the power of God as the great resource in facing the risks.
5. Withdrawal from the mating dance.
6. "Look into one another's eyes: This is the person you are marrying. To program change in another is manipulation."
7. Pressure points: Review in chronological order.

8. Task orientation trap which destroys the present.
9. Preventative medicine: To arm oneself to know what problems might arise.
10. The phenomenon of growth together: The "ladder tree" as compared with growing apart over the years
F. "How do you feel about it all?"—Offer the couple an "out" without shame.
G. The couple's questions and comments about marriage, themselves, the church, etc.

V. Review of the Wedding Service
A. Discuss the wedding service.
  1. Review its theology.
  2. Review its shape.
B. Decide on music and readings.
C. Define roles:
  1. Celebrant.
  2. Bride and groom as the ministers of the sacrament.
D. Discuss eucharist in service as a great starting point for marriage.
E. Set down necessity for rehearsal with everyone present on time and with all their faculties about them.
F. Set down rules for photographer.
G. Close with assurance that should any questions or problems arise, the pastor is anxious to help!

Appendix B
A Household Budget

Income	Yearly	(÷ *12 Monthly*)
Husband's salary	_____	_____
Wife's salary	_____	_____
Investment income	_____	_____
Scholarships	_____	_____
Bonuses	_____	_____
Retirement benefits	_____	_____
Disability benefits	_____	_____
Regular gifts, e.g., from family	_____	_____

Balance in Savings Accounts	_____

Expenses

The Wedding and Related Events:	*Amount*	*Paid by:*
Invitations (including postage)	_____	_____
Church fees		
Clergy	_____	_____
Musicians	_____	_____
Church use fee	_____	_____
Sexton	_____	_____
Or Tithe	_____	_____
Physical examinations		
Bride	_____	_____
Groom	_____	_____
Clothing		
Bride	_____	_____
Groom	_____	_____
Parents	_____	_____

	Amount	Paid by:
Bride's party	_____	_____
Groom's party	_____	_____
Rehearsal party		
Place	_____	_____
Catering	_____	_____
Flowers	_____	_____
Rental car(s)	_____	_____
Photographer	_____	_____
Reception		
Place	_____	_____
Catering	_____	_____
Gifts to wedding party	_____	_____
Additional transportation	_____	_____
Miscellaneous	_____	_____
Honeymoon or wedding trip:		
Trousseau	_____	_____
Travel	_____	_____
Hotel	_____	_____
Meals	_____	_____
Rental car or local transportation	_____	_____
Miscellaneous	_____	_____

(Make certain to indicate who will pay for each of the above expenses, such as the bride's family, groom's family, bride, groom or other person.)

Home:	Yearly	(÷ *12 Monthly*)
Rent/House payments	_____	_____
Taxes	_____	_____
Insurance	_____	_____
Heat (gas, oil, electric)	_____	_____
Electricity	_____	_____
Payments on furnishings and appliances	_____	_____
Anticipated improvements	_____	_____
Water/sewer	_____	_____
Lawn care	_____	_____
Maintenance fees (condominiums)	_____	_____
Phone (basic rate + long distance)	_____	_____
Contingency	_____	_____
Car:		
Loan payment	_____	_____
Gas and oil	_____	_____

	Yearly	(÷ 12) Monthly
Regular maintenance		
Anticipated major repairs		
Garage rental		
Insurance		
Taxes and plates		
Insurance:		
Life		
Husband		
Wife		
Medical–dental		
Household (if not listed above)		
Automobile (if not listed above)		
Personal:		
Food		
Medical		
Dental		
Prescriptions		
Child care		
Clothing		
Work clothes/uniforms		
Commuting expenses (buses, tolls)		
Outstanding debts:		
Balance owed on credit cards		
Balance owed directly to merchants		
Student/educational loans		
Other		
Charitable Contributions:		
Church pledge		
United Fund pledge		
Other		
Savings: Amount you plan to save each month		
Miscellaneous: (The Sneaky Ones!)		
Clubs and organizations fees and dues		
Fees for continuing education		
Books, newspapers, periodicals		
Entertainment; going out—sports events—theater—entertaining friends in your home		
Vacations		

Gifts to one another, family, friends   ——————— ———————
Alimony and child support   ——————— ———————
Hobbies   ——————— ———————
Other expenses unique to your situation: ——————— ———————

  ——————— ———————
  ——————— ———————
  ——————— ———————
  ——————— ———————

Footnotes

Preface
1. Jessie Bernard, *The Future of Marriage* (New York, 1973), p. 301.
2. Robert F. Capon, *Bed and Board* (New York, 1965), p. 21.
3. Carl R. Rogers, *Client-Centered Therapy* (Boston, 1951), p. 20.
4. *Ibid.,* p. 33.

Chapter I
1. *Punch,* June, 21, 1977.
2. Bernard, p. 123.
3. *Marriage, Divorce and the Church, The Report of the Commission on the Christian Doctrine of Marriage* (London, 1971), p. 59.
4. *The Book of Common Prayer* (New York, 1977), pp. 859–860.
5. Paul Tillich, *Systematic Theology, Volume II* (Chicago, 1957), p. 9.
6. *The Book of Common Prayer,* p. 427.
7. *Ibid.,* p. 531.
8. Bernard, *Ibid.*
9. Nena and George O'Neill, *Open Marriage* (New York, 1972).
10. *The Book of Common Prayer,* p. 431.
11. *The Oxford Dictionary of the Christian Church* (New York, 1957), s.v. "Covenant."

Chapter II
1. *The Book of Common Prayer,* p. 423.

Chapter III
1. Harry S. Sullivan, *Conceptions of Modern Psychiatry* (New York, 1953), pp. 42–43.
2. William J. Lederer and Don D. Jackson, *The Mirages of Marriage* (New York, 1968), p. 107.
3. *Ibid.,* pp. 41–59.

4. For these insights, I am deeply indebted to The Rev. Dr. Morton Kelsey, Ms. Barbara Kelsey and to Ms. Melissa Costello whom I heard at a conference in October, 1978, sponsored by the Indiana Newman Foundation and the National Institute for Campus Ministry.

Chapter IV

1. An alternative strategy for testing the couple's ability to deal with communication and conflict is to propose a "role-play" with both reacting as they think they would in a problem situation. The pastor may design his own role-plays within the following guidelines: First, there may be no clear-cut answers, no clear right or wrong; second, the situation must be appropriate to the couple's background, education, etc.; third, if possible, a situation or problem should be drawn so that after a few minutes, the roles may be reversed. Abraham Lincoln offered to debate the issue of slavery with anyone and offered to take either position, thus sharpening his understanding of the reasons and feelings of both sides, on the basis of which he took his final position; fourth, the situation should be chosen keeping in mind that any possibility of the discussion devastating either person is definitely to be avoided—we are not in the business of destroying persons. Quite obviously, this exercise must be used in the final session when both parties are present. Should the pastor identify substantial problems in this area, it may be appropriate to use both techniques.

2. Speed Leas, *Chuch Fights* (Philadelphia, 1973); Manuel J. Smith, *When I Say No I Feel Guilty* (New York, 1975); and George R. Bach and Peter Wyden, *The Intimate Enemy* (New York, 1968).

3. Harvey Cox, *On Not Leaving It to the Snake* (New York, 1969).

4. *Statistical Abstract of the United States 1978, 99th Edition* (Washington, 1978), p. 31.

5. Elizabeth Kübler-Ross, *On Death and Dying* (New York, 1969).

Chapter V

1. For a sobering discussion of this issue, see Adolf Guggenbuhl-Craig, *Power in the Helping Professions* (Zurich, 1978).

2. Harvey Cox, *op. cit.*

3. Sylvia Porter, *"Job Hunting," The Detroit Free Press,* February 18, 1978.

4. *The Book of Common Prayer,* p. 427.

5. *Ibid.,* p. 430.

Chapter VI

1. *Ibid.,* pp. 435–436.
2. *Ibid.,* p. 423.
3. What should one do if someone should stand up and voice objections? I have only heard of two such unfortunate occurrences. On one occasion it was a dispute between a father and a step-father as to who had the right to give the bride away. Clearly, while it was obviously a genuine domestic dispute, it was not just cause for postponing or cancelling the wedding. The second occasion was more complex. In response to the charge to the congregation, a woman at the rear of the church stood and in a clear voice said, "Sir, I do!" The priest asked the woman to come forward and addressing her asked, "Madam, I have but one question to put to you: Will the objections you raise stand up in either an ecclesiastical or civil court?" She answered "They will." The priest asked the congregation to be seated and asked the bride, groom, best man, maid-of-honor and the woman to join him in the vestry. He asked for the specific charge, to which she replied, "This man is my legal husband." The groom admitted that he guessed that he had never quite gotten around to the formality of a divorce. The priest returned to the altar where he simply stated that the marriage would not take place, dismissed the congregation with an appropriate prayer (nervously offered) and returned to minister to a family in sore distress. If the clergy are called upon to ask such a question they should be prepared to respond as well.
4. *Ibid.,* p. 424.
5. *Ibid.,* p. 427.
6. *Ibid.,* p. 425.
7. *Ibid.,* p. 427.

Bibliography

Bach, George R. and Peter Wyden *The Intimate Enemy.* New York: Avon, 1968.

Bailey, Derrick S. *The Man-Woman Relation in Christian Thought.* London: Longmans, 1959.

Bernard, Jessie *The Future of Marriage.* New York: Bantam Press, 1973.

Butterfield, Oliver M. *Sexual Harmony in Marriage.* New York: Emerson, 1953.

Capon, Robert F. *Bed and Board.* New York: Simon & Schuster, 1965.

Cox, Harvey *On Not Leaving It to the Snake.* New York: Macmillan, 1969.

Crane, William E. and J. Henry Coffer, Jr. *A Religious Attitudes Survey.* Family Life Publications, 1964.

Dominian, Jack *Christian Marriage: The Challenge of Change.* London: Longman and Todd, 1967.

Guggenbühl-Craig, Adolph *Power in the Helping Professions.* Zurich: Spring Publications, 1978.

Jaques, Jeffrey M. and Karen J. Chason. *"Cohabitation: Its Impact on Marital Success."* The Family Coordinator, XXVIII (January, 1979), 35-39.

Jones, Cheslyn, editor, *For Better for Worse.* London: The Church Union, 1977.

Kübler-Ross, Elizabeth *On Death and Dying.* New York: Macmillan, 1969.

Leas, Speed *Church Fights.* Philadelphia: Westminster, 1973.

Lederer, William J. and Don D. Jackson *The Mirages of Marriage.* New York: W. W. Norton, 1968.

Lehrman, Nat *Masters and Johnson Explained.* New York: Playboy Press, 1976.

Marriage, Divorce and the Church: The Report of the Commission on the Christian Doctrine of Marriage. London: S.P.C.K., 1971.

New English Bible. Oxford: Oxford University Press, 1970.

Newcomb, Paul R. "Cohabitation in America: An Assessment of Consequences." *Journal of Marriage and the Family,* XLI (August, 1979), 597–603.

O'Neill, Nena and George *Open Marriage.* New York: Avon, 1972.

Oxford Dictionary of the Christian Church, The Edited by F. L. Cross. New York: The Oxford University Press, 1957.

Porter, Sylvia "Job Hunting." *The Detroit Free Press.* February 18, 1978.

The Book of Common Prayer. New York: The Church Hymnal Corporation and The Seabury Press, 1977.

Punch. London: June 21, 1977.

Rogers, Carl R. *Client-Centered Therapy.* Boston: Houghton Mifflin Company, 1951.

Smith, Manuel J. *When I Say No I Feel Guilty.* New York: Bantam, 1975.

Statistical Abstract of the United States 1978, 99th Edition. Washington: United States Bureau of the Census, 1978.

Sullivan, Harry Stack *Conceptions of Modern Psychiatry.* New York: W.W. Norton and Company, 1953.

Tillich, Paul *Systematic Theology: Volume II.* Chicago: The University of Chicago Press, 1957.

NOTE:

Since completing this manuscript, I have come upon two books which I would commend enthusiastically to all premarital counselors. The first is *Kiss Sleeping Beauty Good-bye* by Madonna Kolbenschlag (New York: Doubleday, 1979) and the second, *Toward a New Psychology of Women* by Jean Baker Miller (Boston: Beacon, 1977). The first of these offers well thought out and easily communicated reflections on the role and treatment of women in our society past, present, and future. Kolbenschlag is a Roman Catholic religious, a fine and articulate scholar. The Miller volume is a good companion to *Sleeping Beauty,* as she offers yet another construct which is complementary to Kolbenschlag.